WHAT YOUR
HUSBAND ISN'T
TELLING YOU

WHAT YOUR HUSBAND ISN'T TELLING YOU

A GUIDED TOUR OF A MAN'S
BODY, SOUL, and SPIRIT

DAVID MURROW

BETHANY HOUSE PUBLISHERS

a division of Baker Publishing Group
Minneapolis, Minnesota

© 2012 by David Murrow

Published by Bethany House Publishers
11400 Hampshire Avenue South
Bloomington, Minnesota 55438
www.bethanyhouse.com

Bethany House Publishers is a division of
Baker Publishing Group, Grand Rapids, Michigan

Printed in the United States of America

Library of Congress Cataloging-in-Publication Data
Murrow, David.
    What your husband isn't telling you : a guided tour of a man's body, soul, and spirit / David Murrow.
        p.   cm.
    Includes bibliographical references.
    Summary: "Presents candid insights about the inner world of Christian men, exploring the factors that determine what they say, do, and believe. Covers topics such as communication styles, relationships, sex, fears and motivations, and spirituality. Includes discussion questions for women's small groups"— Provided by publisher.
    ISBN 978-0-7642-1011-2 (pbk. : alk. paper)
    1. Christian men—Psychology. 2. Husbands—Religious life. 3. Husbands—Psychology. 4. Marriage—Religious aspects—Christianity. 5. Wives—Psychology. 6. Man-woman relationships. I. Title.
BV4528.2.M873 2012
248.8′435—dc23   2012028761

The stories of men and women in this book are true. Some names and specific details have been altered to honor privacy.

The Internet addresses, email addresses, and phone numbers in this book are accurate at the time of publication. They are provided as a resource. Baker Publishing Group does not endorse them or vouch for their content or permanence.

In keeping with biblical principles of creation stewardship, Baker Publishing Group advocates the responsible use of our natural resources. As a member of the Green Press Initiative, our company uses recycled paper when possible. The text paper of this book is composed in part of post-consumer waste.

Cover design by Lookout Design, Inc.

Author is represented by WordServe Literary Group

12   13   14   15   16   17   18   7   6   5   4   3   2   1

Contents

Contents

Preface

The Iceberg

A renowned psychologist once compared the human mind to an iceberg. We see only the tip, while the bulk of our thought processes are invisible, submerged in a deep region known as the subconscious. This seems doubly true for men, who tend to be less aware of their feelings than women are.

There are a number of great books that examine the tip of the iceberg. Authors such as Stephen Arterburn and Shaunti Feldhahn have revealed much about men by simply asking them what they think—polling them scientifically and capturing their responses in bestselling books.

But this approach only reveals what men *consciously* think. If the shrinks are right, about 80 percent of a man's thought processes are opaque—even to him.

This is why committed family men suddenly leave their wives for no reason. Why deacons smile at church and then scream at their children in the car all the way home. Why men who are normally wise with money sink their cash into ridiculous Ponzi schemes. Why men who truly love their families suddenly abandon them—if not physically, then emotionally.

Oftentimes men have no idea why they do these things. Your man doesn't know what's going on under the waterline any more than you do.

In this book, we'll examine the tip of the iceberg (what men tell researchers) as well as its vast underside (what men feel but are unwilling or unable to put into words). By looking at the whole iceberg, you will emerge with a complete picture of what motivates your husband to do and think the things he does. Together, these are the things your husband isn't telling you.

Introduction

What's Really Going On Inside Your Husband

Picture your husband standing in the middle of a swiftly flowing river. Every day a steady current of joys, frustrations, compulsions, temptations, and pressures comes flooding downstream and washes over his heart.

It's exhausting work, standing against this current. Some disciplined men are able to do it pretty well. Others try to dam the river—but frustration eventually spills over the top. Some men eventually drown, taken under by pressures and sorrows they cannot fathom.

Most men have no idea where these feelings come from. Many try not to feel anything at all. Some are so skilled at denying their emotions they aren't aware they have any. Rare is the man who knows how to deal with his feelings in a healthy way.

So instead of living fully and freely, the majority of men resort to survival strategies in order to stand against the current. Instead of being honest about what they feel and asking people to meet their needs, they learn destructive, manipulative ways of getting what they want. Game-playing. Displays of anger. Pointless bickering. Destructive behaviors. Habits they can't kick and don't even enjoy. It takes so much energy fighting back the current (or trying to control it) they can't be fully present in the moment. Many simply check out—becoming passive and unavailable to their loved ones. They veg out in front of the TV or computer—not because they don't care, but because there's nothing left to give.

Every man fights these currents. Even the good husbands. Even Christians.

I am such a man.

I'm what you'd call a nice Christian guy. I had it pretty good as a kid—middle-class upbringing, plenty to eat, a roof over my head. I made good grades in school and had lots of friends. But my mom and dad were caught in a spiral of codependence—he was a raging lion and she was a pacifying lamb. Dad was a ticking time bomb—and you could never predict when he would go off. Mom taught us various survival strategies: Don't upset your dad; be quiet; stay in your room; get outside; eat quickly; get good grades; be careful what you say; and most important, always be right.

I gave my life to Christ at age fifteen in large measure because I didn't want to become like my dad. I've been serving Jesus ever since. I went to a Christian university and married a Christian woman. We've been faithful churchgoers and have raised our three kids in Sunday school. God gave me the grace to forgive my father years ago, and when he died we were at peace.

But something still wasn't right.

For decades I did not know my own secrets. I could not explain the crazy dialogue that ran constantly through my head. I had a hard time expressing genuine grief or empathy. At times I felt so overwhelmed I could barely hold everything together. Although I was mostly satisfied with my life, I occasionally fantasized about leaving everything behind—or ending it altogether. A secret death wish lurked just beneath my consciousness.

Then, one year ago, I was taken under. I landed in a residential drug and alcohol treatment program three thousand miles from home. I was cut off from my family. My phone and computer were confiscated. I was placed in an apartment block with seven other men, most of whom were addicts who had lost nearly everything.

Now you're probably wondering, "What did Murrow do? Was he an alcoholic? A druggie? Violent?" Actually, I was none of those things. I've never smoked a cigarette. I've never been drunk or high in my life. Never touched an illegal substance. Never struck my wife or kids. No porn. One hundred percent faithful to my marriage vows.

Nevertheless, I found myself in a rehab program. My self-image as a good husband and better-than-average father lay shattered on the floor of my dorm room.

In times past, I'd have become angry about my false imprisonment. I'd resort to one of my survival strategies to get through the indignity of my situation. I'd tell myself that I was right—and everyone else was wrong. Or I'd try to work the system and gain the upper hand over my captors (in this case, counselors).

But instead, I gave in.

At the age of forty-nine, I finally began the process of meeting the real me. My counselors taught me to begin asking the foundational questions: *What's bothering me? Why do I feel so ignored? Why is there always tension in my house? Why am I so afraid to speak up for my own needs? Why do I feel like I'm disappearing—and another man is taking my place? And why is this happening to a born-again Christian man, who is not supposed to have these kinds of problems?*

In terms of the river analogy, I finally stepped out of the current and climbed onto the bank. And I began the upstream trek to the headwaters of my soul. I went back to the source of my frustrations, wounds, and deadness of heart.

Once I discovered the source, the currents began to make sense. I realized I was still living out my survival strategies from childhood: Be quiet, stay in your room, get outside, eat quickly, be right. I was like a World War II Japanese soldier stranded on a remote island, fighting a war that's been over for decades.

Today the currents still buffet me, but they no longer overwhelm me. I know why I feel the way I do. I know who the real enemy is and how to fight him.

After seeing the change in my heart, my dear wife set off for the headwaters of her own soul. Turns out we were both in denial about how we were really feeling. We're getting healthy together. Instead of playing games or manipulating one another to get our needs met, we speak honestly and openly about what we truly think and feel. I'm finally willing to speak up—and she is finally willing to hear what I'm actually saying. Just as Jesus said, the truth is making us free.

Come with me to the headwaters. I want you to understand the powerful forces that shaped your man, and the currents that roil him every day. I want to teach you how to be honest with your husband as a way of helping him to be honest with you.

This book is so much more than a list of facts about men or the latest research on their attitudes (although I'll be quoting plenty of those). I want you to understand that thing that's bothering him. That thing that's motivating him. That thing that's frightening him. We're going back to the source.

And I do mean the source. For the next few chapters, I'll be taking you back to the dawn of mankind. I'll open the history books to show you how men became the way they are.

At some point you may be wondering, *Why is he explaining tribal customs to me? I just want to know why my husband won't put his dishes in the sink!* Trust me. Your man is the product of thousands of years of cultural development. Modern men have only been modern for the last couple hundred years—but centuries of human experience has shaped who they are. You cannot understand your husband until you see how he and his father and his father's father became men. Please bear with me as I unpack the biblical, historic, and scientific origins of manhood. Once you understand these origins, you'll better understand your husband.

Reality check: If I had the luxury of speaking to you and your husband in person, I could much more accurately diagnose your particular situation. As the author of a book, that's not an option. So I have no choice but to speak in generalities about him. I guarantee that at some point you'll come across passages that are just flat wrong about your husband. You may be tempted to roll your eyes and say, "Murrow doesn't know what he's talking about. My husband is nothing like that!" And you're right. There are some things I'm going to get wrong about your man, because not all men are alike. I'm fully aware that certain men don't fit the norms I describe, and that's a good thing. So please don't dismiss the entire book because of the parts that may not apply to your guy.

You may also feel at some point I'm stereotyping the genders. Try to realize the bind I'm in—I can't very well write a book about men without drawing some general conclusions about them. This is a book about what average guys (Christian and non-Christian) think all the time but never tell their wives. It's a faithful attempt to describe the inner thoughts of the average, mentally stable male in modern Western society. If your husband is seriously disturbed or mentally ill, the principles I share in this book probably won't apply to him. If you're in an abusive relationship, you need far more help than this book can offer.

As you read, you'll probably see lots of things that not only apply to your husband but also to you. Several women who've reviewed this manuscript have said, "David, when you were describing my husband's (fill in the blank), you could have been describing me!" Men and women are wonderfully different, but we fall into the same traps. I hope these pages not only teach you much about your husband but also much about yourself.

And please don't misunderstand: When I describe the quirks of men I'm not saying they *should* be this way. I'm fully aware of how broken and dysfunctional guys can be. My goal is not to make excuses for men. I'm simply telling you what they are thinking but not saying.

I will spend a lot of time describing women behaving badly in this book. Does this make me a woman basher? Absolutely not. But sometimes a woman contributes to her husband's dysfunction without realizing it. As they say, it takes two to tango. You need to know what a man thinks when his wife provokes, disrespects, or mishandles him. I want you to profit from the mistakes other women have made. You may not be able to change your husband, but you can certainly change yourself.

Some books try to help too much. They offer too many specific suggestions. That's not what I'll be doing here. In fact, for the first 80 percent of the book I'll offer almost no advice at all. Don't be frustrated by this. I'm taking Jesus' approach—instead of spoon-feeding you the answers, my goal is to help you ask the right questions. As such, this book is more *descriptive* than *prescriptive*.

Once you gain insight into your husband's inner life, take your concerns to God in prayer. Seek him for the answers. And there is no shortage of very helpful marriage-building material from dozens of talented, experienced Christian authors. I've compiled a list of some of the best at my web address for women, www.speakingofmen.com.

Finally, I want to give you fair warning: This book is a bit like a tour of a sausage factory. I'm going to share some really messy stuff with you. Most of it is not politically correct. I guarantee you will read things that disturb you. If you do not handle this truth properly, it could sow a weed of distrust between you and your husband.

On the other hand, I'm a big believer in the power of the truth. Jesus said that knowing it would make us free. So if you really want to know what your husband isn't telling you, come with me to the headwaters of his soul.

PART ONE

THE FOUNDATION OF MAN AND MANHOOD

Before I take you to the headwaters of your man's soul, we must go back to the very beginning—to the headwaters of mankind.

You're familiar with the story of Adam and Eve? A serpent tempts the woman to eat from the Tree of Knowledge of Good and Evil. She plucks the fruit and hands it to her husband. The two eat, their eyes are opened, and sin enters the world. Paradise lost.

In his anger, God expels the rebellious couple from Eden. But the Creator quickly follows with his first two acts of mercy on behalf of the human race: He *provides* clothing for their bodies. And he *protects* them from further contamination by stationing an angel with a flaming sword at the entrance to the garden.

God *provides*. God *protects*.

Adam was watching. And he, wanting to "be like God," took upon himself these two roles: provider and protector.

Men have been providing and protecting ever since.

Men derive great joy from providing food, clothing, and shelter to their loved ones. Every day, millions of men march off to jobs they'd rather not be doing in order to provide. Providing is more than something men do—it's central to who they are. Most guys would work even if they didn't need the money.

But even deeper is a man's need to protect. Men instinctively protect their families, their property, their honor, and themselves. If a man fails to protect these things, he feels a deep sense of failure.

Modern men have developed multibillion-dollar industries whose sole purpose is to protect people, property, and assets (security, banking, insurance, firearms, industrial safety, etc.). Men organize armies and police forces to protect the citizenry. Even men's favorite sports are built around the protection of a goal area (the end zone, home plate, the net) by trying to keep the other team out.

Some men are wonderfully healthy in these two roles. When your man is secure and balanced as a protector and provider, he's happy. So is everyone around him. Life is good.

But when he's out of balance in one or both, expect trouble. And that leads us to the great problem with men: most are either over- or underdeveloped as providers and protectors. Here's the result:

	Provider	Protector
Underdeveloped	Lazy, slacker	Cowardly, passive
Overdeveloped	Workaholic, greedy, stingy	Defensive, controlling, emotionally remote

I'm convinced that every fear, dysfunction, and insecurity in a man's life flows from either an overdeveloped or underdeveloped need to provide or protect. It's Adam taking his roles too seriously, or not seriously enough.

And this is the gigantic secret your husband's not telling you—because he probably doesn't know it himself. Your husband's need to provide and protect will at times overwhelm his soul. It will be the source of every triumph and folly in his life. It's creating the hidden pressure that causes him to clam up—or to explode. It's keeping him from connecting on an emotional level with others. And it may actually be turning him into someone else.

1

Understanding "Provider"

My name is Provider.

I am that voice in your husband's head that tells him to make sure you and the kids have food, clothing, and shelter. I'm that compulsion that tells him to get up and go to work when he'd rather sleep in. I told him to get an education, to improve his skills, to take the extra overtime, to save and invest—even when he didn't want to do any of those things.

As David told you earlier, I sprang into being at the fall of man. Prior to the fall, God was earth's sole Protector and Provider. But after the fall, as a part of the curse, God commanded Adam to provide and warned him it would be difficult (Genesis 3:17–19). Then God showed Adam how it's done: by providing clothing for his naked children. That's the moment I was born. I whispered into Adam's ear: *See that? It's your job now.*

I've been whispering to men ever since. Good men have always gone to great lengths to provide for their families. In ancient times men picked up spears to hunt dangerous beasts for food. As agriculture took hold, men threw their backs into clearing and cultivating fields. Today men around the world plunge into dark mines, steamy factories, and rat-infested cargo holds to earn enough money to provide for their loved ones.

While some men truly love their work, most would rather be doing something else. A study by the Conference Board research group found that just 45 percent of Americans are happy in their jobs, a record low.[1] A CBS News poll found that a third of U.S. men believe their generation has worse opportunities to succeed than their parents' generation (only a quarter of women felt this way).[2]

Our world is full of men who dislike their jobs—but they trudge to work each day because I tell them to. In David's home state of Alaska, there are thousands of men who toil in the desolate oil fields of the North Slope. They spend a minimum of two weeks on shift, pulling twelve-hour days, hundreds of miles from home. Most men hate spending half their lives away from their loved ones, but the pay is good. Slope work is not about personal pleasure—it's about providing.

Even men who like their jobs have to deal with workplace "stuff" they'd rather avoid. Every guy has at one point or another wished he didn't have to go to work. One of the most beloved country songs of all time goes like this: "Take this job and . . ." You know the rest. Men may fantasize about chucking it all and moving to a tropical island, but very few do. Why? I'm the powerful voice that convinces men to put duty ahead of desire.

Providing is so important that men rank themselves by their careers. Have you noticed what men talk about when they meet?

Levi: Hi, my name is Levi.
Josh: I'm Josh. Nice to meet you.
Levi: So Josh, what do you do?

Levi doesn't even finish the sentence. Josh knows what he's asking: What do you do *for a living*? A man's very definition of himself comes from how he provides. That's me—Provider—doing my job.

In fact, men rank each other by their work. If a man has a prestigious career, other men esteem him higher. When a powerful man walks into the room, we rise to our feet to show respect and admiration. But men who do menial work (or who are unemployed) are often ashamed to tell others. In the film *The Company Men*, Bobby Walker (Ben Affleck) tries to keep his sudden job layoff a secret from everyone, including his wife. He lies to friends and relatives and refuses to cut back on luxuries, even as his financial situation becomes desperate. Bobby would rather lose everything than admit he's unable to provide.

So strong is my voice that men continue to work even when they don't have to. Why do moguls such as Bill Gates, Warren Buffett, and Mark Zuckerberg go in to the office every day, despite having billions in the bank? I give men meaning and purpose. Without me, men flail.

Money, food, clothing, and shelter are not the only things I tell men to provide. I also press them to leave a mark on the world—to provide a legacy to mankind. I tell wealthy men to endow universities and hospitals and to name buildings after themselves. I tell common men to leave an inheritance to their children. In fact, I'm the voice that tells men to bear children—and to stick around and raise them to adulthood. This may surprise you, but if I did not tell men to do this, most would not.

Look at child rearing from a man's perspective. Whereas the sexual act that produces children is pure pleasure for a man, raising them is not. Children compete for his woman's attention. They interrupt his sleep. They make messes. They're expensive. Worst of all, they become *teenagers*. Looking at child rearing through a completely selfish lens, it makes no sense for a man to raise his offspring.

Some men figure this out. Life's a lot more fun with fewer responsibilities and more freedom. So they avoid commitment. They father children out of wedlock. They become deadbeat dads. *Papa was a rolling stone.*

Yet the vast majority of men would never consider doing this, even though child rearing is a huge headache. Why? Because I tell them to stay put and provide.

Here's something your husband isn't telling you: He considers it an honor to provide. That $5K he sank into your daughter's braces? He'd rather have spent it on a boat, but he makes the sacrifice willingly. When a man puts aside his personal happiness in order to provide, I pat him on the back and whisper, "Well done." And a glorious feeling of satisfaction washes over his heart. When your husband provides unselfishly, you have me to thank.

I am Provider—and I'm a relentless taskmaster. My voice cannot be silenced. I keep whispering, even to men who lose their jobs, who become disabled, or who retire. Men who find themselves suddenly unable to provide often descend into despair, depression, or even madness.

Some men are healthy in their provider role. They work hard, but also leave adequate time for fun, family, and faith. They possess ambition, but are not consumed by it. They listen to my voice, but do not grant me total control over their time.

But many, many men are unhealthy providers. The dysfunction manifests itself two ways:

Underdeveloped need to provide: Some men have learned to tune out my whisperings. These are the classic "slacker" men who lack ambition and drive. Their numbers are growing. William Bennett writes:

> In 1970, men earned 60% of all college degrees. In 1980, the figure fell to 50%, and by 2006 it was 43%. . . . [T]oday, 18-to-34-year-old men spend more time playing video games a day than 12-to-17-year-old boys. While women are graduating college and finding good jobs, too many men are not going to work, not getting married, and not raising families.[3]

There's been a steady stream of Hollywood films lampooning slacker men who refuse to grow up. Such films did not exist until recently. Movies such as *Knocked Up* or *Failure to Launch* would not have made sense to the audiences of the 1950s—but today they ring true.

In Japan, a new generation of young men is rejecting their fathers' workaholic, macho ways. Dubbed "herbivore men," these sweet, floppy-haired boys are uninterested in having sexual relationships with women. They like baking and sewing, reading comic books, and spending time with family. They are exceptionally mild and show little interest in building a career. This is a concern in Japan, where both the birthrate and the economy are in the doldrums.[4]

Why are so many men today feeling little urgency to provide, even when given the opportunity to do so? I don't know. I am Provider, not Psychologist. But I can assure you that many men today (particularly younger ones) have learned to drown out my voice. Their lack of ambition is hurting these men and the women who want to love them.

Overdeveloped need to provide: Some men hear my voice too well. These men place outsize emphasis on career, goals, and ambition. This condition was common among men who came of age during the Great Depression. In the late 1960s, a term was coined to describe them: *workaholics*. Such men provide abundantly for their families' material needs, but neglect their relational and spiritual needs.

An overdeveloped need to provide can produce men who are greedy, materialistic, and avaricious. Greed results when a man hears my voice above all others. I can become so loud I drown out the voice of reason, the voice of wisdom, and the voice of God.

Foolish men sink their money into get-rich-quick schemes out of a distorted need to provide. Others pile on huge debt so they can provide their families with unneeded luxuries. They buy homes, cars, and toys they cannot afford in order to keep up with the Joneses, and then find themselves chained to debts they struggle to repay.

Sometimes a woman will amplify my voice, pushing her husband to provide designer clothing, posh home furnishings, and extravagant family vacations. "Honey, we need new granite countertops. They're more sanitary," she purrs. Crafty women know their husbands' need to provide is strong, and they use it to get what they want.

Strangely, some men try to provide by not providing. They become stingy. These men look to the future, gripped by fear that their money will run out and they'll lose their ability to earn more. So they hoard today in order to provide tomorrow. I'm not talking about men who are thrifty or those who prudently save a portion of their income; I'm speaking of men who deny their families the basic necessities of life in order to pile up treasure.

These men not only fail to provide adequately for their families, but they lack generosity with others as well. Americans are the wealthiest people on the planet, yet they give, on average, less than 2 percent of their annual income to charity. And the more a person earns the lower percentage he gives.[5] Many men do not believe the words of Jesus, who tells his children not to worry about tomorrow, that *he* will provide everything to those who seek his kingdom first (see Matthew 6:31–33).

Thank you, Provider. This is David writing again.

So this is what your husband isn't telling you: He feels a deep obligation to provide. The pressure is constant. His social standing and psychological well-being depend on it.

Your man *wants* to provide for you. But it takes a terrible toll on him. It's a constant struggle to know how much to work and how much to rest, what to spend and what to save, whether to quit his soul-killing job in order to follow his lifelong dream. Modern men live under a sword of fear that their jobs will be eliminated, their skills will atrophy, or their contributions will be unwanted.

Provider's voice is strong—but if you really want to understand what's driving your husband, you need to get to know Protector. He introduces himself in the next chapter.

2

Understanding "Protector"

My name is Protector.

Like my counterpart, Provider, I emerged at the fall of man. As Adam was expelled from the garden, he took one last look over his shoulder. There he saw something remarkable—a fearsome angel, wielding a flaming sword, protecting the entrance to Eden.

Adam had never seen anything so powerful. He wanted that power.

So Adam assumed the role of protector—and I was born.

Here's the first thought I placed in Adam's head: *Fashion a weapon, like the one you saw in the angel's hand. You'll need it to protect your family.* So Adam created an offensive weapon. At some point, he undoubtedly showed his son Cain how to wield it—with deadly results.[1]

And that's been the problem with me since the dawn of humanity. I protect life, but I also take it. Under my influence, men have committed acts of incredible virtue and unspeakable evil. I am at once the linchpin of civilization and the rock that crushes it.

I am that part of your husband's soul that springs into action when there's a threat. I'm the instinct that causes him to automatically shield you and the kids when he hears a loud noise. I'm the voice that told him to buy a car with air bags and a weapon for the house.

I am Protector. I am the reason so many men are drawn to military service. Why men become firefighters and police officers. Why every "guy flick" features a hero who protects others. You know their names: James Bond, Ethan Hunt, and Jason Bourne; Neo, Gandalf, and Eli; Maximus, William Wallace, and Captain America—protectors all. I'm the reason 80 percent of the men aboard the *Titanic* perished, while 74 percent of the women survived.

I am the reason comic book heroes are so popular with men. Clark Kent, Bruce Wayne, and Peter Parker are all mild-mannered gentlemen. But when they don their superhero costumes, they're transformed into protectors. These characters represent the secret role every man longs to play. I bring out nobility, courage, and valor in men. But not in every man.

Underdeveloped need to protect: Some men can barely hear my voice. Such fellows become passive, cowardly, and weak. They fail to protect their loved ones. Society has always despised such men. The thesaurus mocks them: *cowardly, lily-livered, fainthearted, spineless, timid, fearful, pusillanimous, weak, feeble, yellow, chicken, weak-kneed, gutless, wimpish, contemptible.*

Overdeveloped need to protect: Other men hear my voice too loudly. They become hyperaggressive and competitive. They can't back away from a fight. It's not enough to win— they must crush their opponent. My voice is particularly dangerous in the ear of a dictator. Deranged leaders have ravaged nations out of a misguided need to protect their people—or their own power.

Which brings us to the biggest thing your husband isn't telling you—the central secret of his heart: The person he protects most is himself.

Your husband learned to protect himself when he was just a wee lad. Something bad happened to him. I came to the rescue. I grabbed the boy and shielded him from the threat. He survived.

As your husband matured, more bad things happened to him. Some were the normal hurts of growing up: A teasing bully. A girlfriend's rejection. Bad grades. Not being picked for the team. And some may have been horrific: Sexual abuse. Abandonment. Starvation. A raging, alcoholic parent.

Every man is wounded as a boy. Whether these hurts are big or small isn't the issue. Here's what you need to understand: From a young age, I taught your husband to protect himself. I showed him how to endure the pain and how to survive similar situations in the future. I told him to get up, dust himself off, and keep going. I taught him phrases like "That's water under the bridge"; "It's not that bad"; and "Big boys don't cry." I kept him alive when he wanted to die.

Each time your husband was hurt, I took a part of his heart and locked it away in a safe place so it could never be damaged again. Over the years I secured more and more of his heart. The more he was hurt, the more of his heart I protected.

Eventually, your husband became disconnected from his true heart. He no longer had access to it, because it was locked away in a cage. He even began to forget the things that had hurt him so deeply.

Over the years your true husband began to disappear, and I took his place. I am the false self he projects to the world.

I am Iron Man, the suit of armor that makes your husband impervious to the missiles that sail toward him all day. The suit keeps hurts out, but it also traps emotions inside. These emotions simmer, boil, and occasionally explode, scalding those around him.

I am Protector. I am the sum of your husband's survival strategies: Boasting. Hiding. Humor. Drinking. Career. Addiction. Hobbies. Success. Sports. Sarcasm. Bigotry. Silence. Machismo. Revenge. Guilt. Wealth. Rage. Control. There are as many survival strategies as there are men. I am the hidden hand behind them all.

Now, about that little boy. Each time I locked away a part of his heart, it stopped growing at that point—frozen in time. For example, if your husband was hurt often as a youngster, then there is a part of his heart that's still three or four years old locked deep inside. If he was wounded as a teen, he may be emotionally frozen in adolescence. If he went off to war and witnessed its horrors, he may have come home a different man. That different man is me—Protector. I keep men alive—but at great cost.

Your true husband may occasionally slip his cage and give you a glimpse. He may come out if his favorite team wins a game, if things go well at work, or after he's had a couple of drinks. Sometimes he shows up during sex, sports, or a movie.

Why do men crave their addictions? Drugs and alcohol put me, Protector, to sleep. While I'm dozing, the little boy can escape and play for a few minutes. This is why men under the influence often act like children. Chemicals can sometimes release that part of their hearts that's frozen in childhood or adolescence.

Ahhh. He feels good. The pain is gone. So he drinks some more. The child suddenly finds himself in control of a man's body with all its powers and passions. And it frightens him.

The anger at his captivity and the pain of his wounds surface. Protector awakens. I swing my sword indiscriminately through the fog of his intoxication. In a drunken rage I can destroy everything and everyone around me.

Your husband's problem isn't the alcohol or the drugs or the porn or the fantasy football or the job or the money. He's using these things in a vain attempt to release the boy from his cage. Hear me: Your true husband is a boy who wants to play again. He wants to live pure and free. But he is imprisoned by forces he cannot comprehend. Most men do not recognize their own captivity.

How can men be freed? Jesus said, "Truly I tell you, unless you change and become like little children, you will never enter the kingdom of heaven" (Matthew 18:3–5).

Look at that verse in the context of what I'm telling you. Christ says that unless a grown man becomes like a child, he will not enter into all that God has for him.

So how can a man become like a child? By visiting the headwaters of his soul. He must go back in time to his childhood, to mourn the wounds and hurts that imprisoned him in the first place. He must revisit the bad stuff, bring it to the surface, and allow Christ to take those wounds onto himself.

Jesus said, "Blessed are those who mourn, for they will be comforted" (Matthew 5:4). Mourning can be a difficult process. Men don't do it very well. It forces a man to become weak, vulnerable, and real. It inevitably involves crying and hugs, which modern men are not supposed to do.

But once the mourning and comforting takes place, your husband's wounds will begin to heal. His need for self-protection will slowly melt away. He'll learn how to get his needs met in a healthy way. At that point, I have no choice but to lower my sword and let the boy out of his cage.

The man who emerges will be the one you truly love; the one you saw during courtship. The one who looked at you with such affection on your wedding day. The one who knows how to laugh and play and have fun. The one who is not only willing to die for you but is willing to *live* for you.

This is David writing again.

I have a friend who emerged from his cage about a year ago. Let's call him Stan. He attended a men's weekend sponsored by The Crucible Project. He went at the urging of a friend who told him little other than "It changed my life. You've gotta go."

Stan was expecting the typical Christian men's retreat: sing a few songs, listen to a speaker, shoot some baskets, eat fatty foods. But from the moment he arrived at the retreat center, he knew something was different. Men stood up and shared from the heart—stories of how they had slipped their cages and found freedom.

Stan sat in the back row with arms folded across his chest. Protector was screaming at him: *There's nothing wrong with you. You're already a Christian. You don't need this stuff. You are NOT going to cry.*

Later that evening, two men engaged Stan in conversation. They began asking pointed, difficult questions—on topics men rarely discuss but are desperate to talk about. Stan was sweating—with fear or excitement, he wasn't sure.

These men offered to take Stan back to the headwaters; to revisit the painful moment when his heart was locked away—abused in a way no child should ever be. Stan agreed to go. There they found the boy, sitting in a cage, where he had been imprisoned for three decades. Over the course of the weekend, these men smashed the cage Protector had built around young Stan, and led him out into the sunlight for the first time in thirty years.

Freedom!

Stan had never experienced such joy. His heart was light. He was walking on a cloud. Even the colors that met his eyes were more vibrant. Although he had been a Christian for many years, he felt as though he had been born again—again. It was his first taste of abundant life.

When Stan came home, he reintroduced himself to his wife (we'll call her Tammy). "You don't know me," he said. "The man you've been married to all these years doesn't exist. I'm here now, and I'm deeply in love with you." What followed was a mind-blowing season of confession, repentance, tears, reconciliation, and ultimately, a much healthier marriage. Tammy loved the old Stan, but she's crazy about the new one. Everything—and I do mean *everything*—is better at Stan and Tammy's house.

⌇

According to the gospel of Luke, here's the first thing Jesus says about himself:

> The Spirit of the Lord is on me, because he has anointed me to proclaim good news to the poor. He has sent me to proclaim freedom for the prisoners and recovery of sight for the blind, to set the oppressed free, to proclaim the year of the Lord's favor. (4:18–19)

This is Christ's mission statement—the topic sentence of his ministry. He came to set captives free. Even those who have imprisoned themselves in a cage of self-protection.

And here's the coolest part: Once your husband stops needing to protect himself, he will have the energy to truly protect you and the kids. And then, over time, his circle of protection will widen to include the extended family. And then widows, the poor, and the weak. He'll become the kind of protector this world desperately needs.

But he cannot begin to protect others until he stops protecting himself.

Dear reader, you cannot free your husband from his cage. Only Christ can. And he usually accomplishes this work with the help of strong men. Men who know their way to the headwaters. Men who are not afraid to break open cages and set captives free. I keep a list of organizations that do this kind of work on my website for women: www.speakingofmen.com.

Part 5 of this book explains how men gain freedom from the cage of self-protection. In between here and there we're going to examine how Protector and Provider influence just about everything your man thinks, says, and does. In the next chapter, we'll travel back in time to see how the art of providing and protecting are rapidly changing in our modern world—and how men are struggling to keep up with these changes.

3

How Providing and Protecting Have Changed

Men need to provide and protect. Yet today's men are feeling insecure and uncertain in these roles.

A lot of men are being left behind in the new economy. Gender roles that were clear for centuries are now murky. Male behaviors that were once welcomed by society are now sneered at. The Western world is experiencing unprecedented peace and abundance, yet men are mysteriously adrift. Men still possess energy and drive, but are having a difficult time finding an acceptable place to exert it.

Your husband deals with these upheavals at some level—if not consciously, then under the waterline. Headlines about mass layoffs make him nervous. The masculinity of his father's generation has been dismissed as sexist and patriarchal but nothing has emerged to take its place. Social structures that supported men for centuries are dissolving away.

Before we dive in, let me say this in the strongest possible terms: I am not blaming women for the change in men's roles. Advances in technology are driving the loss of male power and influence. Women are simply filling the void left by these changes. It is wrong for men to blame women for their change in status. After all, men are the primary creators of this brave new world.

However, my job is to tell you what your man is really thinking and feeling—justified or not. You need to understand why so many men think the rug is being pulled from under their feet—and why some men feel that women are doing the pulling.

Climb into the time machine with me as we pay a visit to the earliest peoples. We'll take a quick tour through the history of providing and protecting, and show you how remarkably these have changed in the past two hundred years.

Since the dawn of the species, humans have been locked in a life-and-death struggle to feed themselves and to fend off invaders. It's hard for us in twenty-first-century Western society to imagine how hungry and violent the world was until recently. Famine was common. Crop failures routinely killed thousands. Hordes regularly swept through settlements, sacking, raping, and pillaging at will (the Old Testament is full of these accounts). There were no standing armies, police forces, or welfare programs to prevent this suffering.

Men were indispensable in earlier times because they possessed the physical strength to raise crops, hunt animals, and fight wars. It's no exaggeration to say that men held the key to the survival of the human race. If men failed to hunt or farm, women and children starved. If men failed to protect, women and children were slaughtered. If men didn't do their jobs, all was lost. No men = no hope.

Men have always done society's dangerous jobs. Humans never even thought of giving these roles to women until recently because females are physically weaker than men. Women were needed to bear, raise, and protect children. Men were the "expendable sex"—and so were assigned the jobs that were most likely to kill someone.

But one day, a tribesman got wise. "Why should I hunt beasts that can rip my flesh?" he asked. "Why shouldn't I run away when a superior enemy threatens? When I'm hungry, why shouldn't I eat all the food myself, instead of sharing with the rest of the tribe?"

The leaders of the tribe panicked. "If this kind of thinking spreads through the tribe, we're finished! We need a way of motivating men to overcome their natural fears so they will become the protectors and providers everyone needs."

So the leaders hatched a plan. "We'll play a trick on the men," they said. "We'll create a code of manly behavior, and we'll expect every man to obey it."

So tribes all over the world developed various versions of the code of manly behavior. Among the expectations of the code:

- A man is strong.
- A man is brave in the face of danger.
- A man endures suffering.
- A man puts the needs of others first.
- A man is generous.
- A man leaves a legacy.

The code of manliness helps a man overcome his natural instincts (fear, hunger, loneliness), so he will do what's best for the tribe, not for himself. The code convinces men to do things that have the potential to hurt, exhaust, or kill them.

Societies made sure every man understood the code. Ado-
lescent boys were subjected to brutal coming-of-age rituals
to ensure the code was implanted deep in their hearts. Men
who lived up to these expectations were rewarded. They got
the best homes, the most wives, and the choicest foods. They
were given the name *hero,* and their exploits were memo-
rialized in songs. They got medals and parades when they
returned from war.

But men who failed to act manly were shunned as cowards.
They were treated as outcasts by society.

So for thousands of years humans all over the globe fa-
vored men in order to motivate them to do the dangerous
jobs. Men were given an elevated place in society, including
rights and privileges unavailable to women and children.
Patriarchal societies survived longer because their men were
more motivated to sacrifice themselves; egalitarian societies
tended to die out. For five thousand years, sexism equaled
survival.

Contrary to modern belief, men didn't seize power from
women in order to oppress them. Women gave their power
over to men in exchange for food and protection. Here's the
ancient bargain women struck with men: *Guys, we'll let you
lead the parade, in exchange for the promise that you will
feed me and the kids, and die for us if necessary. I'll take the
domestic sphere; you take everything else.*

And they did. Men have always dominated government,
commerce, and academia. They owned most of the property, controlled most of the wealth, and cast all the votes.
Inheritances passed through sons, not daughters. Kings took
precedence over queens. Men made the big decisions, women
lived with the consequences.

And for five thousand years that arrangement seemed acceptable to most humans. It's still the way things are done
in half the world.

But then everything began to change—quickly. Set the time machine for AD 1800. A novel technology—the internal combustion engine—gave birth to the Industrial Revolution. A new kind of society was born, one that completely changed how humans protect and provide for themselves. Suddenly, for the first time in history, men were no longer indispensable.

How industrialization changed providing: With the rise of machinery, raw muscle power became much less important. Farm implements allowed one man to do the work of twenty. Advances in science increased crop yields dramatically. Never before had food been so abundant, easy to acquire, and relatively cheap compared to income.

Industrialization severed the visible link between men and food production. Today's kids no longer see their fathers bringing home a kill or a crop. Instead, food comes from a store, gathered by their mothers. Children's strong association between father and providing began weakening with industrialism.

Industrialized countries became wealthy enough to create a social safety net. Women could now rely on government welfare programs instead of husbands as their primary providers. Education and vocational opportunities for women multiplied, which increased their income and decreased their dependence on men.

How industrialization changed protecting: In prehistoric times, every man was a warrior—literally. Rival bands frequently raided each other's camps. Every man was expected to pick up his weapon and repel the invaders. In the age of agriculture, farmers grabbed their implements and went to war to defend their homelands. The Old Testament is replete with stories of kings mustering common men to fight the Caananites, the Ammonites, the Amalekites, and various other *ites* who threatened the nation of Israel.

But in the past 150 years, the role of protector has gradually been taken away from common men and given to professionals. The wealth created by industrialization funded the rise of professional, full-time armies and navies. Municipalities established the first public, salaried police forces and fire departments in the 1800s.

As a result, modern men rarely have to defend themselves. The average American male will go his entire life without using a weapon to physically protect his family or property. In some nations it's illegal to own a gun for self-protection. Battle is becoming rare even among professional soldiers. Fewer than half the U.S. veterans alive today saw combat during their military careers.[1]

Thanks to industrialization, a relatively small number of men can provide us with all the protection we need. Around the world armies are shrinking because one warrior can wield the power of thousands. Never was this more apparent than on August 6, 1945. Twelve men aboard the *Enola Gay* killed an estimated 130,000 people and leveled the city of Hiroshima in a matter of minutes. Battle machinery such as tanks, planes, bombs, and machine guns have greatly amplified the power of one soldier.

The same is true with providing—today we need only a few men to feed us. In 1800, 90 percent of the U.S. labor force was engaged in farming. It took that many hands to sustain our populace. Two hundred years later, U.S. population has grown more than fifty-fold, yet only about 2 percent of Americans work as farmers.

Machines enabled women to become professional protectors and providers for the first time. A female fighter pilot is just as lethal as a male one. Put a woman behind the wheel of a combine and she can harvest just as much wheat as a man. Physical power is no longer key to the survival of the human race—brainpower is.

Men have lost their traditional advantage as protectors and providers for society. I'm not suggesting society turn back the clock so men can regain their dominance. I'm merely pointing out how quickly industrialization has removed men from their indispensable role as the linchpin of society. Men just aren't as important as they once were. Suddenly society can get along quite well with just a handful of them.

This change in men's importance did not go unnoticed by women. In the mid-1800s, a few of them looked around and realized their survival no longer depended on being married to a protector and provider male.

These women became known as feminists. Their movement began at the Seneca Falls Convention in July 1848. Feminists had a radical message: *Women and men should be treated as equals. Discrimination against women makes no sense.*

Society scoffed. For five thousand years men had been on top—and for good reason. Feminist pioneers such as Lucretia Mott and Elizabeth Cady Stanton were considered insane for questioning the superiority of men.

But slowly feminist ideas gained traction because they made sense in a world where men were no longer the key to humanity's survival. Western women began to question the ancient bargain. "If I don't need him to die for me anymore, why am I giving him all the power? If I can feed and clothe the kids without him, why should I submit myself to him and his gender?" Why indeed?

Female power bloomed during the twentieth century. Women got the vote in 1920. During World War II, Rosie the Riveter proved that a machine-powered woman was just as effective as a machine-powered man. The feminist movement of the 1960s and '70s swept away the last major strongholds of male power and prerogative. Women were granted full banking and property rights. Military units, colleges, and workplaces were gender integrated. Newspapers of the 1970s carried weekly stories about "The First Woman to _____ (fill in the blank)." Title IX expanded the role of women in sports.

For centuries, men gathered in all-male enclaves such as lodges, card rooms, and country clubs. But in the 1980s, women stormed into all-male organizations such as Rotary and Kiwanis clubs. Men-only gathering spaces dwindled. The social structures that supported male camaraderie have eroded or have become mixed-gender. As a result, men have never been more friendless. We're all Marlboro men—riding the High Plains alone. We've lost our esteemed place in society, and we're out on our horses looking for it.

In a little less than 200 years, society went from lauding men's accomplishments to holding them in contempt, particularly among the intelligentsia. The PC crowd sneers at men who fight wars, men who carry guns, men who cut down trees, and men who drill for oil. We no longer expect men to subdue the earth. Instead they're supposed to live in harmony with it.

The feminist storyline has metastasized from "equal rights for women" to "men are the oppressors of women." There's a great deal of hatred and suspicion directed toward men on university campuses. It's just assumed that men are responsible for every modern ill: war, environmental degradation, economic inequality, and the exploitation of various victim groups. If only women were in charge, we'd be living in a peaceful, egalitarian eco-paradise, so their thinking goes.

Men are no longer society's greatest asset; they are its biggest problem. Each day men become a little less necessary. Guys sense this, and as their value diminishes we see them withdrawing from the workforce, the church, civic organizations, and from public life in general.

Don't be fooled—just because a few powerful men still control the worlds of business and government, this does not mean that common men are just as empowered as they once were. For every David Beckham or Rupert Murdoch or Barack Obama, there are millions of men who are being left behind as we transition to the Information Age. It's no coincidence that the retailing giant of the new era—Amazon.com—shares its name with a mythic race of female conquerors.

So even as millions of women question the ancient bargain (*Why should I give him the power if I don't need him anymore?*), so do men (*Why should I sacrifice everything for her and the kids?*). Society is quickly moving toward complete gender autonomy. Some see this as progress, but it's creating a lot of lonely women, isolated men, and fatherless children.

Dr. John Gray said, "Not to be needed is a slow death for a man." We're witnessing the early symptoms of that death in our society today:

Addiction. Men of every race suffer addiction, but no population has been harder hit than Native American males. These men stand just two or three generations removed from their hunter-gatherer forebears—esteemed warriors who served as protectors and providers for their people. No other population of men has been stripped so quickly of its essential role in society—and the consequences have been devastating.

Suicide. Once again, Native men suffer the most. Young Native men take their lives at rates almost twice that of men of other races.[2] Here in Alaska, suicide is the leading cause of death among Native men ages twenty to twenty-nine. But it's not just Natives—men of all races take their own lives at four times the rate of women. Men who feel useless are quick to exit the stage.

Pornography. Men's pornography use is not about sex. It's about being needed, looked up to, and desired. It's about having power over a woman. Every man's sexual fantasy involves a woman who desperately needs him. Now that women no longer need men, the multibillion-dollar Internet porn business has stepped in to fill the void. Sex websites provide online harems of cyber women who whisper, "I need you so badly," to their paying clients. Men feel the momentary rush of pleasure that comes from being needed by a woman—even though she and her affections don't really exist.

Don't take this wrong—I'm not blaming you if your husband is interested in porn. Here's my point: As society and women need men less, more guys will turn to anything that makes them feel needed. Even something that's harmful, expensive, and illusory.

Passivity. Men's roles used to be clearly defined. Men were doctors; women were nurses. Men were executives; women were secretaries. Men were athletes; women were cheerleaders. It was easy for men to declare their masculinity by their jobs, hobbies, and interests.

These days everyone does everything. Our gender-blind society has left men no way to define themselves as uniquely male. This is one reason today's young men are refusing to step up—or are engaging in extremely risky, antisocial behaviors. They're saying to the world, "Look at me! No woman would take the risks I am taking."

Entertainment addiction. Many men are getting lost in sports, movies, and video gaming. These cathartic experiences allow men to feel the thrill of battle without anyone actually getting hurt. Video games are particularly addictive—players are given a big gun and the role of protector. They get to save the world and repel hordes of digital bad guys, without shedding any real blood. It's a chance to feel strong and necessary again.

Australian journalist Irina Dunn famously said, "A woman needs a man like a fish needs a bicycle." In some ways she's right: A modern woman no longer needs one special guy; she has armies to protect her, government to provide for her, and artificial insemination to give her children. For the first time in human history, a woman can have it all without linking herself to a man.

Once again, I'm not blaming women for any of this. Nor am I blaming you. I'm not seeking your pity on behalf of men. I merely want you to see how much men's value to society has fallen—and how quickly it fell. *The Atlantic* magazine published an article titled "The End of Men":

> Earlier this year [2010], women became the majority of the workforce for the first time in U.S. history. Most managers are now women too. And for every two men who get a college degree this year, three women will do the same. For years, women's progress has been cast as a struggle for equality. But what if equality isn't the end point? What if modern, postindustrial society is simply better suited to women?[3]

Humanity is now in the early stages of a fourth wave—the Information Age. In a world dominated by ideas, physical power means nothing. Brainpower means everything. And whose brain is better suited to this new world? We'll see in chapter 4.

PART TWO

UNDERSTANDING YOUR HUSBAND'S BODY

In a manner of speaking, you are married to three men. Humans, created in the image of God, are body, soul, and spirit.

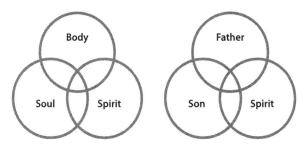

Each person forms a trinity, just as God does.

If you're really going to know your man, you must know his body, his soul, and his spirit. For a couple to be truly one, they must experience intimacy on all three levels.

There's a tragic misconception among Christian women that when a man's spirit is renewed, his body is too. These women think: *Well, he's a Christian now. That must mean his fleshly desires will disappear. His lusts will fade. He'll crave God's Word instead of cigarettes. He'll start eating right and stop slurping his soup.*

Ladies, here's the truth: Even after a spiritual awakening, a man's brain, hormones, and body chemistry remain the same. When we receive Christ, our spirit is redeemed, but the battle for our souls and bodies has just begun.

Because humans are social and spiritual creatures, we tend to forget or deny the strong role biology plays in our earthly existence. Example: Your husband is irritable for no apparent reason. You might assume he's under spiritual attack, when in reality he's just hungry. Instead of praying for your husband, it might be far more effective to fix him a sandwich.

If you really want to know your man, you need to get to know his body. Let's start at the top: the mysterious male brain. Then we'll work our way down to where it really gets interesting.

4

Understanding the Male Brain

I have a friend named Mark Gungor. He's a comedian who masquerades as a pastor in the city of my birth: Green Bay, Wisconsin.

In addition to leading the largest congregation in the smallest football town in America, he conducts a seminar called "Laugh Your Way to a Better Marriage." His seminars are so funny they are causing men to go temporarily insane:

> *Man: Sweetheart, I've got a surprise for you.*
> *Woman: Ooh, what is it? Flowers? Chocolate?*
> *Man: Something better. It's two tickets to a marriage seminar. I thought we could spend some time working on our relationship.*
> *Woman: (Walks slowly over to the phone and dials 9-1-1.) Hello? Police? I have a strange man in my house!*

One of Mark's funniest sessions is "A Tale of Two Brains." Turns out modern brain scans have revealed significant differences inside the heads of men and women (did we really need science to tell us this?). I won't recount his entire comedy routine here, but among the facts he cites are these:

- A human brain has two hemispheres. The left side is home to the logic and reasoning centers of the brain. The right side is home to emotions, feelings, intuition, and social relationships. Gungor says the bulk of men are left-brained logical types, whereas the majority of women are right-brained emotive types.
- Men tend to be better at analyzing systems, while women tend to be better at reading the emotions of other people.
- Although the male brain is larger, the female brain has more connections between cells, which means women are able to use their brains more efficiently than men do.
- Women have a much bigger connecting structure between the two hemispheres, which allows them to move information more freely from one side to another. Men's hemispheres don't work nearly so well together.
- The regions of a woman's brain that are devoted to language are larger than those in a man's brain. This tends to make them better talkers and readers. (A recent study found that 55 percent of women read literary works for pleasure, while only 38 percent of men do.[1])
- Men have larger amygdalae, a pair of tiny glands at the base of the brain. Whenever a person has a highly emotional or frightening experience, the memory is stored in the amygdalae. This may explain why men have a greater fight-or-flight impulse and why men flash back to horrific events in their lives more frequently and vividly than women do.

Brain differences start in the womb. In utero, boys experience a wash of testosterone between eighteen and twenty-six weeks of gestation, which actually damages the connections between the two hemispheres, making them more independent of each other. (Hah, you knew men were brain-damaged!) As Gungor puts it, "Men are born to think unilaterally. We think in either the right or left hemisphere, but seldom in both at the same time."[2]

This bifurcation of the male brain makes it harder for men to do things that require interaction between the hemispheres, such as reading, expressing feelings with words, and managing emotions. Your husband *can* do these things, but not as easily as you can.

This is why most men need peace and quiet at home in order to think straight. If there's a loud TV blaring or a baby wailing nearby, their brains literally lock up. All their gray matter is dealing with the distraction, leaving them unable to process anything else.

Have you ever wondered why the most logic-driven man can become completely irrational when his emotions rise? Because most men can function optimally on only one side of the brain at a time, if a man becomes enraged, it's as if his logic-processing unit is temporarily shut off. Senseless babble comes out of his mouth and his fists start swinging because the left side of his brain is inaccessible. A few minutes later he cools down and can think rationally again because his emotions are in check and his left brain is back online.

Return to the womb. In utero, the female hormone estrogen actually encourages the development of connections between the hemispheres. So a woman gains superior links that allow her to easily process information on both sides of her brain simultaneously. Gungor writes,

> Hence, women are more in touch with their feelings and can more easily express them than men can. They have an increased ability to bond and be connected to others. This

is why women are the primary caretakers for children. There is no society on earth where men take on this role. Because of brain difference women have a more acute sense of smell, better hearing, and keener eyesight than men do.[3]

Feeling pretty good about yourself? You should. God made you wonderfully different from your husband—and gave you many advantages.

The female brain is also better at multitasking. Women are vastly superior at juggling multiple jobs, deadlines, and stimuli. My wife is a master juggler. She can simultaneously cook dinner, listen to the radio, answer the door, restrain the dog, break up fighting siblings, and conduct an Internet search, all while counseling a friend over the phone.

Speaking of the phone, have you noticed the differences in how men and women use this device? My conversations with friends often sound like this:

Hey, what's up? (pause) Yeah, I'm going. How 'bout you? (pause) Sure. I can give you a ride. (pause) Okay, see you at 6:30. Bye.

For men, a telephone conversation is a way of conveying a specific piece of information. Once that information has been transmitted, the call is over. But not for women. If I were to write out the transcript for one of my wife's conversations, it would consume the rest of this book. She often goes into triple-overtime with friends, discussing issues from every possible angle. When I take her to task for her lengthy jabbering, she winks at me and says, "Why use ten words when a hundred will do?"

Technology has not leveled the playing field for males. A few years ago, when my eldest children were in the fifth and seventh grades, instant messaging was the rage. I would frequently observe them chatting with friends over the computer. My son, the seventh grader, would often have just one chat window open, whereas my daughter, the fifth grader, would frequently engage in ten conversations at once, all neatly tiled across her screen.

A study from the Pew Research Center found that the average teenage girl in the United States sends or receives eighty text messages from her mobile device in a day, compared to just thirty for the average boy. Girls are more likely to have long exchanges with friends, more likely to text about schoolwork, and more likely to send a message "just to say hello" several times a day.[4]

While the majority of computer users are men, women dominate digital social networks such as Facebook. They are more likely to post photos to their profiles and comment on others' statuses. Men use social networks to share funny videos and informational links more frequently than women do.[5]

All these differences can be traced back to the way our brains work. Bill and Pam Farrel put it this way: Men are like waffles; women are like spaghetti. They write:

> Men process life in boxes. The typical man lives in one box at a time and one box only. When he is at work, he is at work. When he is in the garage tinkering, he is in the garage tinkering. When he is watching TV, he is simply watching TV. That is why he looks as though he is in a trance and can ignore everything else going on around him. Social scientists call this compartmentalizing—that is, putting life and responsibilities into different compartments.[6]

When a man is in a particular box, it's as if the other boxes don't exist. He forgets completely about them. Whatever a man is focused on *right now* gets 100 percent of his attention. If he's watching a tight football game on TV and the sofa catches fire, he may not even smell smoke. There's another name for this: tunnel vision.

Mark Gungor has his own take on the boxes metaphor. He says, "There's a box for the job, a box for the wife, a box for the kids, a box for the money, a box for the mother-in-law (taped up and stuffed somewhere in the basement), et cetera."

According to Gungor, the most important box to a man is his Nothing Box. That's right, men have a box with nothing in it. And it happens to be a man's favorite box. He would spend all his time there if he could. When you see a man vegging out in front of the TV, fishing but not catching, or lying in a hammock staring at the sky, he's in his Nothing Box.

Women don't have a Nothing Box. Women are always thinking about something.

> Woman: *Honey, what are you thinking about?*
> Man: *Oh, nothing.*
> Woman: *(thinking)* He's lying. He's hiding something from me.

No, he's not lying. He's not hiding anything. Men really can think about nothing. And we love it.

In fact, our Nothing Box is one of the main ways we deal with the pressures of being a man. It's into this box we go to escape the crushing expectations of modern life, the multiple demands on our time, the feelings we don't know how to deal with, and the relentless prodding of Protector and Provider. It's an island in the great river of emotion and pressure that washes over our hearts daily. Allow your man to spend a little time each day in his Nothing Box and he'll love you for it.

Have you read *The Strange Case of Dr. Jekyll and Mr. Hyde?* Spoiler alert: the novel's surprise ending comes when an upstanding physician and a vicious murderer are found to be the same man.

Every day our modern media uncover the Mr. Hydes among us: ministers and coaches accused of molestation, pro-family politicians involved in sexual trysts, community leaders embezzling millions. These hypocrites are almost always men.

I have a friend who was married to a Dr. Jekyll. Her husband was a successful entrepreneur, a faithful churchgoer, and an amazing father to their kids. But a few years ago he began to change. He started working out obsessively, disappearing for hours at a time, and wanting less sex. Eventually the truth came out: Her "godly" husband was actually Mr. Hyde. He was involved with multiple women. He had been taking money from their company to finance drugs and prostitutes. He was hooked on porn and had even dabbled in group sex. All the while he never missed a Sunday in church.

You may be wondering how such a depraved man could sit in the sanctuary and hear the gospel each week without coming under conviction. Chalk it up to the compartmentalized male brain. Tom Davis writes about a Christian friend who was a Mr. Hyde:

> Any part of his life could be placed in a compartment . . . untouched by the other areas of life—women, drugs, marriage, church, God. He convinced himself he could go to church and feel the presence of God and feel good about himself. One compartment. Then he would do whatever he wanted the next day. Another compartment. And never feeling guilt.[7]

Psychologists have marveled at how otherwise good men succumb to evil. The foot soldiers of Hitler's Third Reich were common farmers, factory workers, and merchants. Most were family men. Some were even churchgoers. While some served der Führer out of fear for their lives, others got caught up in

Hitler's vision. They were able to place the evils of Nazism in a box separate from their consciences.

Now, let's tie all this brain stuff in with what we learned about men in the previous chapter. In case you skipped or forgot it, here's a brief summary:

In the hunter-gatherer era, men's lives revolved around two responsibilities: hunting for food (providing) and waging war against rival bands (protecting). Their boxes looked like this:

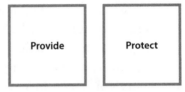

As societies moved into agriculture, men's lives became a bit more complex. Planning ahead became important. Men had to store wealth and protect assets. There were drought, pests, neighbors, government, and organized crime to deal with. Still, men did well under agriculture because their choices were limited. They followed their fathers into the same profession. They ate the same foods and wore the same clothes every day. They rarely traveled far from where they were born. They had about six boxes to manage, and it suited them fine.

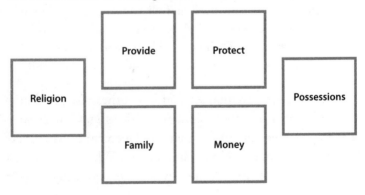

At the dawn of industrialization, men did even better. Most jobs required a single skill. Every man had a favorite beer, a favorite team, and a favorite hobby. There were three TV networks and a handful of radio stations for entertainment. Vacations meant loading the kids into the backseat and driving to see the folks in Ohio. Men had about ten boxes to manage, which was just about their limit.

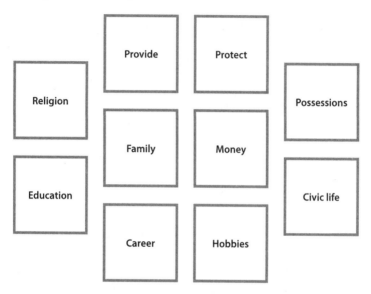

Then came the Information Age. Today's men have dozens if not hundreds of different boxes on their shelves. And each box has within it many subdivisions. Men no longer perform one task at work—even simple jobs require them to possess many skills and juggle multiple deadlines.

The World Wide Web is changing the nature of work. It can be done at any time from anywhere. Every businessperson is supposed to keep a blog, a website, and maintain hundreds of relationships via social networking. We make billionaires of men who produce things you can't even touch.

Many men would love to slow down, but they feel that if they don't keep working at a breakneck pace their jobs could be outsourced to China—or be given to some MBA whiz kid for half the pay. U.S. companies have never been leaner on staff, which forces existing employees to shoulder more of the workload.

Our hunter-gatherer ancestors developed a natural working cycle: plan–hunt–celebrate–rest. Our farmer forebears modified this a bit: plan–plant–harvest–celebrate–rest. Even our factory worker grandfathers found a regular work rhythm—work hard, and when the whistle blows, rest. But in our modern world, work never ends. There's no finish line. The hunter never has the pleasure of standing over his kill.

What leisure time we have is becoming complex. Dozens of activities compete for free time. Hundreds of TV channels and millions of web pages vie for our limited attention. Downtime is a thing of the past. Men are forgetting what it's like to be bored.

So here's what your husband isn't telling you: Thousands of years of conditioning has prepared his brain to focus on one thing at a time—to find it, kill it, bring it home, and then rest. But that's not the world we're living in today.

Who is prepared for this brave new world? Women. You are expert plate-spinners. You are used to being on call. As the old saying goes, "A man may work from sun to sun, but a woman's work is never done." Women have been preparing for our new 24–7 world for millennia.

As a result, we see the attendant rise in female education, employment, and achievement. Companies have noticed women's versatility and work ethic and are hiring them in greater numbers. Men are like landline telephones—reliable machines that do one thing well. Women are like smartphones—sleek multitasking devices that may occasionally drop a call, but can do so much more.

Sure, there will always be gifted men like Steve Jobs whose brains can handle the complexity of our multitasking world. These brilliant men will continue to lead our companies, universities, and governments. But such men are the exceptions that prove the rule. The majority of men lack the brain connections to master the many demands of modern life. It's not that men are dumb—many are simply ill-equipped for the complex society we are creating.

Even if your husband is a pretty good multitasker, he may at times feel overwhelmed by life's many demands. Increasingly, modern society is asking men to perform tasks they are biologically incapable of. Men are waffles in a world that's turning to spaghetti.

So men do what they've always done when they're afraid: They climb into their cages of self-protection. Or they sift through their boxes and pick out their favorite diversion or survival strategy and retreat into it.

I'm guessing a few of you are a bit uncomfortable with the trajectory of this conversation. Since I'm blaming your husband's brain for some of his unpleasantness, does that somehow give him a pass? Am I saying that a man simply can't help his selfish desires? That his brain chemistry made him do it? No, I'm not. Self-control is a basic human virtue, and a fruit of the Spirit. Retreating into self-protection or dysfunction is a choice, and men are responsible for the choices they make.

But you need to know the truth about the male brain and the role it plays in your husband's behavior. You'll never be happy with your man or your marriage until you learn to accept the things you cannot change about him. No amount of prayer, prodding, or protest will change a man's gray matter. (If you think it's tough being married to a man, try marrying a woman.)

Men are this way because they are not women. They are men. What you see as male flaws may actually be a part of God's grand plan for the human race. While you may be hoping God will change your challenging husband, did you ever consider God may be using your challenging husband to change you?

5

Mr. T—The Stuff That Makes Your Man a Man

It's a well-worn trope of sci-fi movies: A brilliant scientist is injected with a chemical that's supposed to give him superpowers. And it works. But those abilities come at a terrible price. The scientist slowly transforms into a monster, consumed by the very powers he sought.

I'm here to tell you that magic chemical *does* exist. It's at work right now in your man's body. It's called *testosterone,* or simply *T.*

Testosterone gives men superpowers—but it can also turn them into monsters. T helps men be bold, courageous, assertive, heroic, and athletic. But it also contributes to men's risk taking, anger, sexual obsessions, and a host of antisocial behaviors. T helps fill prisons, bordellos, stadiums, and barracks.

Both men's and women's bodies produce T, but men typically produce ten to twenty times more testosterone than women do. It's associated with dominance, physicality, and self-esteem. Put two men in a boxing ring, boardroom, or billiard parlor, and the man with the most T usually wins.

If you inject a woman with high levels of T she will begin to take on the characteristics of a man. Her voice will deepen, she'll begin growing facial hair, and her muscles will grow. Her sex drive will rise dramatically. Some women who inject T even develop male-pattern baldness.

T has the same effect in the animal kingdom. For example, among zebra finches only the males sing. Curious scientists injected female finches with testosterone. Bingo—the ladies began chirping. Stanford researchers altered the testosterone levels of lab rats. The female rats developed male genitalia and tried to have sex with their sister rats. Male rats who were denied T saw their genitals wither and they became submissive to other male rats (and to the female rats who thought they were male).

The "he hormone" is responsible for most of what we regard as typical manly behavior. It makes men aggressive, fidgety, and competitive. It drives their legendary interest in sex. T is the fuel that powers economies, builds cities, and ignites wars.

But testosterone is not destiny.

Testosterone level affects behavior, but behavior also affects a person's testosterone level. In a *New York Times Magazine* article, Andrew Sullivan wrote, "Testosterone is highly susceptible to environment. T levels can rise and fall depending on external circumstances—short term and long term. Testosterone is usually elevated in response to confrontational situations—a street fight, a marital spat, a presidential debate—or in highly charged sexual environments, like a strip bar or a pornographic website. It can also be raised permanently in continuously combative environments, like war, although it can also be suddenly lowered by stress."

Tennis players actually see their T levels rise and fall as they win or lose games within a set. One study found sports fans' T levels rose when their team won, but fell when they lost.[1]

Testosterone level spikes twice in a man's life: first in the womb, at about six weeks of gestation. The second spike occurs during puberty. This is no surprise to anyone who's raised a teenage boy. Testosterone turns sweet, adorable ten-year-olds into smelly, swaggering teens. Elevated T drives young men's obsessions with sex, risk taking, physicality, violence, and competition. With all that T sloshing around in their bodies, young men just can't seem to sit still, back down from a fight, or pay much attention during an hour-long lecture in school.

T level begins to moderate during adulthood, slowly declining with age. As testosterone leaves the body, men typically experience decreases in muscle and bone mass, physical strength, and endurance. As T decreases, so does a man's interest in sex and the frequency of sexual thoughts. Erectile dysfunction is a common side effect of decreased T, and drug makers have turned this natural occurrence into a multimillion-dollar business. (Has anyone seen my glasses? I can't find my Viagra!) Low T can even affect a man's cognitive skills and memory and can increase his level of coronary artery disease.

So what does all this mean for you and your husband?

First, understand that T level is important, but it's just one of many factors that affect him. Aggression (or lack of it) is not always a direct result of a man's T count. Psychological, environmental, and physiological factors often play important roles in men's behavior.

Some men use testosterone as an excuse for boorish or sinful behavior. "I'm a man—I can't help it," the saying goes. Malarkey. Many men with high T levels manage to control their desires, just as many men with low T compete at a high level in sports and business. Different people have different levels of the hormone, and they learn to deal with its effects. But this much is true: High T men will have to work harder on their self-control than low T men will. Conversely, low T men will probably experience less motivation and drive, and may have to train themselves to be more assertive.

If your husband is in his twenties or early thirties, he will probably crave physical activity and exercise more than you do, thanks to T. Young men absolutely need to move around and work out. They are naturally more fidgety than women and have a hard time sitting still for long periods of time without a break. As T levels decline with age, so does a man's get-up-and-go.

Young husbands carry about twenty times more T than young wives, so they tend to be more interested in sex than their beloveds, and they desire it more frequently. This is normal. Here's the good news: As the two of you approach forty, your libidos will probably even out. A woman's sex drive increases as she approaches menopause (*tick-tick-tick*), while a man's moderates.

As your husband's T levels decrease over time, you may notice a few positives. He'll probably exhibit increased self-control. His personality may mellow. He may become more introspective and emotive. Hopefully his lusts will subside and he'll only have eyes for you.

But your husband will probably see his declining T as mostly negative. He will lose many of the attributes that define him as a man. Physical stamina—weakened. Waistline—expanded. Work ethic—diminished. Energy—depleted. Motivation—limited. Sexual potency—waning. Worst of all, he will become invisible to women. Waitresses who used to flirt with him at the coffee shop will ask him if he qualifies for the senior discount.

And this is what your husband isn't telling you: He mourns these losses. He knows it's just a part of life, but he's not happy about it. He needs understanding as he adjusts to the fact that he's no longer young, powerful, and immortal. Most men force themselves not to think about their own physical declines. They fail to take reasonable steps to stem their deterioration (diet, exercise, etc.) because it's easier to be in denial, which is the most common symptom of self-protection.

Even if men were willing to talk about their loss of vigor, who would listen? Men generally don't share their weaknesses and fears with one another. Rare is the man who would say to one of his friends, "Hey, I'm having trouble concentrating at work. I'm falling behind the younger guys." Men even avoid talking to their doctors about "old guy" issues such as baldness, erectile dysfunction, and frequent urination because of the stigma attached. To admit that he is losing his strength is a huge psychological blow to a man.

So if he can't talk to his friends and won't talk to his doctor, maybe your husband will talk to *you* about his declining performance? Not a chance. Most men do not like to admit weaknesses to their wives for a number of reasons. Here are three: (1) It's very important to your husband that you see him as strong, competent, and in control; (2) he's afraid you might worry if he admits he's losing his edge; and (3) he's certainly not going to tell you he misses the attention of younger women.

One man put it this way: "If I told my wife I was feeling unmotivated at work, she might think I'm lazy, or she might freak out and think we're going to end up impoverished. I know one guy who was honest with his wife about his struggles at work and within a year she had left him for a wealthy physician. So I just keep these things to myself and pretend nothing is changing. Well, everything is changing and I don't know what to do about it."

Here's what a lot of men do about it: the male midlife crisis.

Typically a man in his forties or fifties notices the effects of his decreasing T level. He begins secretly longing for those pre-married days when life was simpler, responsibilities were lighter, thrills were common, health was perfect, and possibilities were limitless. He also remembers enjoying the attentions of multiple women. Naturally he begins to fantasize about a return to that halcyon era.

For a lot of men, fantasy is where it ends. Or they choose a relatively benign way to live out their dreams. They trade their reliable old minivan for a convertible. They become obsessed with sports or outdoor pursuits. They buy that motorcycle they've always wanted. Some join a geezer rock band or launch a new career. (This is what I did. I published my first book at age forty-four.)

But occasionally a middle-aged man will revert to the irrational, hormone-driven risk taker he was as a teen—only this time he's more dangerous because he's got money. He joins a gym, a tanning salon, and a hair club for men. He buys the toys. He abandons his wife and children and hooks up with a woman twenty-five years his junior. It's all a desperate attempt to prove to his peers (and to himself) he's still "got it."

Dear reader: If your husband left you due to a midlife crisis, please understand that his decision may have had very little to do with you. It's amazing how often men stray from wives they love—women they still find beautiful, sexy, and charming. We need to recognize the midlife affair for what it is: the classic fool's bargain. The devil whispers: *All these things I will give you (back) if you fall down and worship me.* It's not long until these men realize they've lost everything they held dear.

This is what happened to John Edwards, the 2004 U.S. vice-presidential nominee. Edwards was a rising star, handsome, and articulate. Many expected him to be president one day.

But he threw it all away by having an affair with a campaign videographer. In a moment of utter insanity, he allowed her to shoot a professional-quality tape of them in the midst of coitus. She got pregnant. The tape was leaked to the media. In less than a week, Edwards lost his marriage, his family, his reputation, and his career.

Why do men drive themselves over this cliff? Many reasons, but testosterone is the gasoline that fuels the insanity.

This is not a new problem. King David's midlife crisis began when he saw a beautiful woman bathing on a rooftop. Their illicit liaison led to a child, which led to a murder, which led to a cover-up, which led to a public rebuke, which led to a nonstop cycle of violence, rape, rebellion, and exile for David and his family.

King David had more than a dozen wives and concubines to select from. Why did he choose to have sex with a woman who was not his own? Hear me: A midlife extramarital affair is rarely about sex or love. It's about power. A married man who pursues another woman is trying to recapture the vanishing strength of his youth. Ironically, the most powerful men seem to feel the most powerless as the testosterone drains from their bodies.

So why will an otherwise rational man trade everything for a little sex? Why did David, "a man after God's own heart," jeopardize his kingdom for a few minutes of pleasure? It's time to call an expert witness to the stand: Provider. He'll explain the complex relationship between men and sex in our next chapter.

6

Men and Sex

My name is Provider.

David summoned me once again to explain to you why men are so preoccupied with sex, and why women generally are less so.

The very first command God gave his children was this: *Be fruitful and multiply.* Adam took that job very seriously—and he still does today. In fact, God gave the exact same command to animals (Genesis 1:22) and humans (Genesis 1:28). He told them both, *be fruitful and multiply* (NKJV). This biological imperative is hardwired into every living creature. The urge to reproduce is strong and necessary for the preservation of each species.

I've been prodding men to be fruitful since the beginning. This was the scene moments after Adam and Eve were expelled from Eden:

> Eve: *Darling, we're homeless. We have nothing to eat. We've been condemned to a life of hard labor,*

in every sense of the word. We have to learn to wear clothes. And there's a scary-looking angel threatening us with a flaming sword! What should we do?

Adam: How about sex?

You laugh, but that's exactly what happened. The very next verse after the fall of man says: *Now Adam knew Eve his wife, and she conceived.* For men, sex is the solution to every problem. Why do men believe this? Because I remind them to have sex many times a day.

Here's something you must understand about me, Provider. I am like a computer that was programmed long ago. And I run a very simple program with just two instructions: (1) I tell men to provide material goods for their families; (2) I tell men to provide children to the world by having as much sex as possible.

I was programmed this way because in Adam and Eve's day the world was seriously underpopulated. Extramarital sex wasn't an issue because, well, who else were Adam and Eve going to sleep with?

The problem is my program has never been updated. Thousands of years later I'm still telling the sons of Adam to have as much sex as possible with every woman of childbearing age they meet. That's right—if your husband sees an attractive woman who looks like she could bear him a child, a fleeting thought passes through his mind: *Have sex with her.* That's my doing. Your husband can no more control my voice than he can control the wind. I whisper to all men, married and unmarried—Christian and non-Christian.

So here we are in the twenty-first century. Seven billion people inhabit Planet Earth. Many scientists say the world is overpopulated. Yet my original program is still running in the minds of more than three billion men: *Find a woman and have sex with her. Provide children to a world that desperately needs them.*

Now, to look at this from a scientific perspective, I'll hand the keyboard back to David.

Thank you, Provider.

Before the 1800s, humans were relatively scarce in most places on the globe. Populations were small. People dropped dead all the time. Large families were valued because many children died before reaching adulthood. Entire civilizations were routinely wiped off the map by disease, starvation, or warfare—or simply vanished for reasons unknown.

The only way to ensure the survival of the human race was to have lots of children. And the only way to get lots of children was for adults of childbearing age to have lots of sex. Copulation = population.

Somebody had to be the initiator of sex. God gave men more testosterone so they would be thinking about sex 24–7. That's important because it's relatively difficult for women to get pregnant. It can only happen certain days of the month, when conditions are right. God made men libidinous so they would initiate sex frequently. The more often a couple has sex, the more likely they are to have sex at the right time for conception.

A man's powerful sex drive is not the result of sin. The command "Be fruitful and multiply" came before the fall. Sex is the match that ignites the flame that keeps our species alive.

Of course, men's insatiable sexual appetite has obvious downsides. It causes men to be promiscuous. Promiscuity can spread disease and promote poverty. And it's particularly risky for women, since intercourse has the potential to result in a child. Having a child out of wedlock was a death sentence in many societies. Without a husband, a woman had no way to feed herself and her offspring, other than begging or prostitution. The widow of Zarephath in 1 Kings 17 was a righteous woman willing to starve herself and her young son in order to remain faithful to God.

Since uncontrolled sex has always had the potential to result in starving women and children, civilizations began placing sex behind a series of locked gates. Society said, "Want to have sex? Fine, you have to pass through our gates. And we hold the keys. Play by our rules and you can have all the sex you want. Violate our rules and we will punish you."

The most prominent of these gates was marriage. The union of a woman to a man for life was codified and elevated as society's ideal, enforced by every religious tradition (including our own). Marriage betrothed a woman and her children to one man who agreed to protect and provide for them. It stabilized families and formalized inheritances.

Next, society built additional gates to keep people from having sex outside marriage.[1] Adultery and fornication became criminal offenses, punishable by death in many societies. (Adultery is still illegal in about a third of U.S. states, although these laws are rarely enforced today.) As polygamy fell out of favor, bigamy became illegal. Religious codes prescribed total sexual abstinence outside of marriage.

Societies came up with fables to help men resist the powerful allure of women. The legend of the sirens (mermaids) reminded sailors that the beauty and song of a female could lure a man to his death.[2] One of the most common characters in literature and film is the *femme fatale,* an attractive woman who leads an unsuspecting man to destruction.

During the Victorian era, ever-higher gates were built to help men resist temptation. Women covered their arms and legs in public, even when swimming. Pornography and prostitution were made illegal. Dates were chaperoned. Many Victorian men never saw a woman's thigh until their wedding night.

The gates survived into the 1950s. Only married people could rent a hotel room. Condoms were kept behind the drugstore counter. Movies upheld high standards of virtue. TV couples like Ricky and Lucy slept in separate twin beds.

But beginning in the 1960s, the Western world underwent a transformation known as the Sexual Revolution. In a single generation, thousands of years of accumulated sexual mores, rules, and expectations went out the window.

All the gates were opened at once. Why? Oral birth control and abortion-on-demand all but eliminated the risk of an unwanted pregnancy. Moreover, Western nations guaranteed the survival of illegitimate children through newly minted social welfare programs.

Society looked at the gates we'd placed in front of sex and asked, "Why are these here? The risk is gone. An out-of-wedlock birth is no longer a death sentence for women and children. We can plan parenthood now."

Society immediately began relaxing the rules that had kept sex under wraps. One by one, the gates swung open. Soon, the world was awash in sexual imagery—and that's making life difficult for men who want to follow Jesus.

Ours is the first generation in human history with so much sexual stimulation. It's everywhere. You can't walk through a shopping mall without seeing lightly dressed women—or images of seminude models striking salacious poses in store-front windows. Take a dip in a community pool and you'll witness a parade of pubescent girls with bodies 80 percent exposed. Visit a high school (or even some churches) and you'll see a greater variety of female skin in an hour than the average Victorian gentleman saw in a lifetime.

Modern media amplifies the effect. Radio banter is heavily sexual in nature—as are many hit songs. Cable TV is stocked with sexually charged dramas, films, and reality shows. Even news channels bombard men with a steady stream of anatomically impossible female reporters who somehow manage to squeeze their surgically enhanced DDs into size-2 dresses. Men can't even check out at the grocery store without being tempted by racks of gorgeous sirens calling to them from the covers of magazines.

Speaking of magazines, pornography is no longer stashed behind a counter at the convenience store—it's as close as your personal computer screen. Men now have access to thousands of images of nude women with digitally enhanced bodies. And with video streaming, these images have come to life, acting out sexual fantasies men didn't know they had. All it takes is a broadband connection and a credit card. Don't have a computer? You can now access sex on your smartphone— porn in your pocket.

Even legitimate websites are stocked with tempting images of women. Take the social networking site Facebook. I'll be clicking through a friend's profile, and suddenly BOOM. He's posted a picture of his family's beach vacation, including his shapely daughter in a bikini top. I look away from the image, only to see a smiling, gorgeous woman I don't know at the top of his friend list. So I click away from that page, to be greeted by another attractive woman smiling up at me from a banner ad on my Yahoo! homepage.

A hundred years ago a male factory worker might go all week without ever seeing a pretty gal. Sailors would go months without gazing on the female countenance. But today's men see dozens or even hundreds of attractive women every day— both live and in media.

Women, please understand: This is a completely new phase in the human experience. No generation of men has ever had so many images of alluring women served to them everywhere they look. Today's level of temptation and sexual stimulation is completely unprecedented. And your husband is poorly equipped to handle it.

Imagine you are an alcoholic. You come from a family of alcoholics reaching back a hundred generations. All your associates know your weakness, so they're careful not to offer you a drink. The larger society helps you resist by passing laws that restrict the use of alcohol.

But over time your friends forget how vulnerable you are. They begin leaving beer bottles around the house. They serve wine with dinner. They sip cocktails with dessert. They're careful not to offer you one—but they think nothing of boozing in your presence. Furthermore, the price of alcoholic beverages plummets. Drinks become cheap and plentiful. Liquor laws are eliminated. Drinking is everywhere. Even children are allowed to imbibe.

Do you think it might be harder to stay sober in such a world?

Now you understand the level of sexual temptation modern men deal with every day. Western society has forgotten how powerful the allure of sex is to men. And we've stopped making any effort to shield men from it. Modernists equate any suggestion that women dress more modestly with Taliban-like oppression.

This is what your husband isn't telling you: He's under constant temptation by a nonstop parade of sexually charged images. The male brain is not designed to handle this much stimulation. Furthermore, your husband cannot go anywhere to escape these images. The more flesh a man sees, the more Provider calls to him.

Your husband is caught in a squeeze: On one side are his body and the media, telling him to have lots of sex with as many women as he can. On the other side are you and God, telling him to remain faithful to one woman for life. Fifty years ago the media was on your side, but during the 1970s it switched to the have-as-much-sex-as-possible side. Movies and TV shows used to reinforce traditional moral values; today they actively undermine them. Government is moving this direction as well, loosening or abandoning laws that supported fidelity within a man–woman marriage.

I'll say it again: No previous generation of men has ever had to deal with this much sexual temptation in so many different forms. All the gates are open. Anything is possible—particularly for wealthy and powerful men, such as golfer Tiger Woods. Although his multiple adulteries are inexcusable, they are understandable in the context of the life he lives. As one of the world's most famous men, women were fairly throwing themselves at his feet. Society no longer takes marriage vows seriously. The course was open, and Tiger played through. He'll deal with the consequences the rest of his life.

But enough about Mr. Woods. How does this temptation play out in the lives of everyday husbands? Most of the time, nothing physical comes of it. Just 28 percent of married men (and 18 percent of married women) admit to at least one episode of infidelity during the course of their marriages.[3] Almost three-quarters of married men stay faithful to their vows. In our sex-soaked culture this should be regarded as something of a miracle. Society has handed men the keys to the liquor cabinet, and 72 percent are refusing to drink.

But that does not mean they don't look longingly at the bottles.

Here's something your husband isn't telling you: He checks out women all the time. At work. At school. At the store. And yes, even at church.

We'll untangle this vine in our next chapter.

7

What "Men Are Visual" Means

Author Shaunti Feldhahn asked four hundred men this hypothetical question: "Imagine you are sitting alone in a train station and a woman with a great body walks by and stands in a nearby line. What is your reaction to the woman?" Ninety-eight percent of men admitted they would look. (I think the other 2 percent were either gay or lying.)

These four hundred men weren't notorious sinners. Many were churchgoing, Christian men. Yes, God's sons ogle pretty young things.

Feldhahn summarizes her findings this way: "Men can't *not* want to look at a beautiful woman."[1] The desire itself rises unbidden. There's no stopping it. All they can hope to do is control their response.

When I was about thirteen years old, my family and I attended the Minnesota State Fair. I was completely unprepared for what I encountered—a virtual smorgasbord of beautiful farmers' daughters of Nordic descent. I'd never seen so much blond hair, so many blue eyes, or so many perfectly tanned female bodies in one place. That day I developed a lifelong fascination with the tube top.

There was one young lady in particular who really caught my eye. She was traveling in a pack of four girls who were a bit older than I. They were all good-looking, but she was Venus. This girl was more thrilling than the Tilt-A-Whirl and more scrumptious than a funnel cake. So I just followed her at a distance for about thirty minutes. I couldn't take my eyes off her. I dreamt of being her boyfriend. Best I can tell she never even knew I was there. Eventually my parents caught up with me, so I broke off my pursuit. When my mom asked what I'd been doing, I made up a story. I was embarrassed by my obsession. But the image of her perfect face and form were with me for years (though it eventually faded).

Feldhahn calls this "sexual hunting." Men do it naturally. It's our natural desire to find a woman to mate with, programmed into our brains and bodies. It's driven by testosterone and whispered to us by Provider. Men are constantly on the lookout for a healthy young maiden of childbearing age who can carry our genes into the next generation. It's the raw, biological imperative behind the biblical command to be fruitful and multiply. A man's marital status does not affect this urge one iota. Even if a guy has a loving wife and a great sex life at home, his body still tells him to mate with multiple women.

Why is it so hard for a fellow to resist the urge to stare at a beautiful woman? A study from Harvard University found that "when men were shown images of gorgeous female faces, their brain image scans showed that the 'reward' circuitry was activated." The researchers equated the intensity of the effect to the feeling a man gets from using cocaine.[2]

Society used to keep this cocaine under wraps, but now it's available free on every corner, on every screen, and in every magazine. And it's constantly stimulating an area of men's brains known for addiction. Is it any wonder we have so many men getting hooked on porn? We set men loose in the candy store and now we're surprised they're getting fat.

Here's something your husband hasn't told you: The moment he enters a new space, he begins sexual hunting. His eyes scan the area. He looks for the most attractive woman. Then he fixates on her. All the other women disappear. He steals glances her way. Each time he sees her he gets an electrical charge in the reward center of his brain. The mini-cocaine shot. If the woman looks back at him, the shot is more intense. If she smiles at him, his neurons start smoking. If she walks up and speaks to him, his brain turns to jelly and he's unable to say anything intelligent.

When a woman starts flirting with a man, he gets a feeling in his gut. I call it "the tingles." It's the first stage of infatuation. This is when Provider starts whispering questions: *Do I really like this one? Does she like me? What's the possibility of our being together?* I've learned that the tingles are a danger zone for me. I have a strategy: As soon as I experience the tingles, I quickly begin talking about my wife and kids. This usually extinguishes any interest the woman may have in me, and it puts my mind back where it should be.

But still, I hunt. I've been in the grocery store, pushing my cart past the frozen food section. Suddenly I hear the modern mating call—the *clip-clop* of high heels. It's coming from the produce section. I nonchalantly wheel my cart past the potatoes—and there she is. Statuesque. Stunning. *Cocaine shot 1.* I take a second look. She's dressed professionally. Hair coiffed. Probably picking up a few healthy veggies on her way to the gym, judging by that physique. *Cocaine shot 2.* I note her position and plan a route that will take me past her. Slowly I approach, making furtive glances as she thumps a cantaloupe. Soon I'm no more than a meter from the goddess, close enough to detect the mild scent of perfume. Then I roll on by. *Cocaine shot 3.* The rest of the time I'm in the store, I'm aware of her presence and I welcome any additional opportunities to gaze upon her again.

Are you shocked by this? Disappointed? Do you think I'm a creep or a stalker? No, I'm just a regular guy. Your husband has probably done the same thing. Ask him.

Let me answer the questions that are surfacing in your mind:

1. *Does this happen all the time?* Yes. Men always look at women. They always pick out a favorite.
2. *The whole pursuit-with-the-shopping-cart-thing—does that happen every time?* Heavens no. If it did men would never do anything else. That scenario in the grocery store—it's rare. And as I get older it happens less and less (my T level must be dropping). I may not always pursue, but I always look. So do 98 percent of my brothers.
3. *Is this why my husband nearly ran the car off the road when a woman jogged past?* Yes. He was trying to peek at her without your knowing about it.
4. *Do you feel good about this obsession?* No. I hate it. Some crass guys make their lusts public with wolf whistles or catcalls. But most men tend to be embarrassed by them. We try to keep our glances secret. For Christian men, it's actually tiring—a constant battle to maintain purity of the mind. We'd rather it didn't happen, but it's impossible to stop it.
5. *Does this mean you don't find your wife attractive?* Not on your life! My wife is the most desirable woman on the planet. I think she's a fox (sorry, I just had a '70s flashback there). But men are sexual hunters—and I've already captured Gina. My hormones constantly tell me to spread my seed to other women. I despise this

about myself, but the urges come to me uninvited (more on this in a minute).

6. *Does your wife know about this?* She does now.

7. *What's going through your mind when you see a goddess out in public?* Most of the time my thoughts are benign. I'm simply admiring a beautiful woman. I'm not imagining myself in bed with her. I'm just enjoying the pleasure of observing something beautiful—much as I would enjoy looking at a sunset, a work of art, or a fine automobile. But the pleasure of spotting a beautiful woman is more primal and intense because it's linked to the survival of the human race.

Confession time: There have been instances when I've seen a beautiful woman and I've imagined myself with her—particularly when I was younger. Like all men, I've undressed women in my mind. I'm guilty of adultery in my heart (Matthew 5:28).

Because I'm a Christian, I try diligently not to jump from looking to lusting. I'm thankful the task continues to get easier. That's partly because of reduced T, but also because I've been resisting lustful thinking for decades. Years ago I received some very frank (and frightening) teaching on the effects of porn, and with God's help I have not used it in more than twenty-five years. As a result, that area of my brain is trained not to seek stimulation. Each time I feel desire for another woman I recall James 4:7—"Resist the devil, and he will flee from you." That usually does the trick. Sexual thoughts are like any other addiction: The more you give in, the deeper the need becomes. But the more you resist, the easier it is to resist.

And now the final shocker: One of the best places for men to ogle women is in church. That's right—church is a prime sexual hunting ground.

You're thinking: *Ick. Lust in church? I feel like taking a bath . . .*

Sorry to disappoint you, ladies, but men do not check their testosterone at the church door. And churches are target-rich environments (the average U.S. congregation is 61 percent female). It's a roomful of approachable women all looking their best. They're friendly. And they smile at you, even if you're fat, bald, and socially awkward. Some even hug you.

Some women don't make things any easier. You'd think that church would be the one place where men could worship without temptation, but not anymore. The short skirts, tight-fitting blouses, and peekaboo cleavage that made MTV famous are now on display at a church near you.

It's frustrating. Some young churchwomen dress like prostitutes and then complain when Christian men treat them disrespectfully. Get a clue, ladies. You're dangling a Hershey bar in front of a chocoholic and then fussing when he tries to take a bite! If you want chastity, show some modesty. Help men—don't tempt them.

Men's attraction to women is natural and healthy. It's not satanic—it's biological. Here, I'll prove it to you.

If men just wanted to have sex, they'd be attracted to every woman they see. But they're not. Men are only attracted to healthy women in their childbearing years.

A psychologically balanced thirty-year-old male will not want to copulate with an eight-year-old girl. Neither will he find an eighty-eight-year-old woman attractive. Having intercourse with a great-grandmother or a child would not result in a pregnancy, so our bodies do not crave it. The very notion is disgusting to men—and rightly so.

However, that eight-year-old girl becomes very attractive at age eighteen. That's because she is now fertile. Women reach peak fertility in their twenties. And what do you know—that's also the decade when women are recognized as being the most alluring.

Women know this as well. Practically every gal on earth is striving to look like she's in her twenties. Why do women spend billions each year on weight loss, plastic surgery, hair coloring, and makeup? Every woman is trying to appear as if she's in her peak fertility years. That makes her attractive to men—and the envy of other women. There's even a fashion retailer whose very name encapsulates this fantasy—Forever 21.

A few years ago my wife decided to let her hair go gray. Men instantly stopped noticing her. Women treated her with less respect. So she got out the Clairol, and like magic both men and women gave her more attention.

Men are attracted to healthy, fertile women. Their hormones tell them to mate with the women who have the highest chance of bearing children and raising them to adulthood. Our very definitions of beauty come from fertility and survivability. Let's start at the top and work our way down the female body:

Attribute of Female Beauty	Suggests . . .
Lustrous hair, clear skin, rosy cheeks, and full lips	Overall health, survivability
Large eyes, symmetrical face	Ability to see well, find food, and keep track of children
Narrow, long nose (Northern peoples)	Warms the cold air, lessening the possibility of disease
Broad, flat nose (Equatorial peoples)	Aids airflow to the lungs, increasing physical endurance
Good teeth	Ability to chew a wide variety of foods and process nutrients; fend off attackers
Large breasts	Ability to suckle infants

Attribute of Female Beauty	Suggests . . .
Flat stomach	Not already pregnant (a candidate to become pregnant)
Wide hips	Easier for children to pass through birth canal
Long, slender legs	Ability to walk great distances in search of food, and to run from danger
Not overweight	Ability to carry children over long distances

If humans had developed in a different world, it's entirely possible Rosie O'Donnell would be our definition of a supermodel—or we'd see a seventy-eight-year-old woman on the cover of *Cosmopolitan*. But in this world, it ain't gonna happen, because beauty and fertility are so closely linked. Our very definition of a desirable woman is this: healthy and fertile. Women of all ages know this, so they play along.

Have you ever been surfing the Web when suddenly an annoying pop-up ad takes over your screen? You try closing it but another one takes its place. You practically have to shut down your computer to get rid of the thing.

Here's something your husband isn't telling you: He battles erotic "pop-ups" all the time. He'll be sitting at his desk, working hard, when suddenly a sexual image or thought pops up in his mind. Just like a computer pop-up, your husband did not request this thought. It simply appeared. He didn't want it. It's annoying to him. He may try to banish it, but it keeps popping up again.

The pop-ups come from a man's sexual scrapbook. Sorry to tell you this, but every man has one.

When a man sees a sexy woman or a pornographic image, it gets filed in his scrapbook. If a man has sexual relations with a woman, memories of that encounter are stored there as well. So are sexual fantasies. Some men actively collect these mental images to be recalled later. For other men the images seem to deposit and recall themselves.

In times past, the scrapbook was relatively thin for most men. Before 1900, photographic pornography was expensive and rare. The only way a man could see a woman in the nude was to marry her (or pay for a night with a prostitute). But thanks to modern media, men's scrapbooks are bulging with images, movie scenes, and personal memories.

Most men hate these pop-ups and would love nothing more than to be rid of them. Given the choice, men would burn their scrapbooks. Counselor Stephen Arterburn writes, "I have spoken with innumerable men who would like nothing better than to be free from the never-ending barrage of sexual fantasies they entertain."[3]

Women find this hard to believe because they don't keep a sexual scrapbook. The other night my wife and I were watching the comic-inspired film *Thor*. At one point the title character removed his shirt, revealing a body that made mine look like a Popsicle stick. The next day I asked my wife if she could recall a mental image of Thor. "No," she said. She remembered that he was quite good-looking, but there was no picture of the Norse god stored in her brain.

My wife doesn't have a scrapbook—but I sure do. It's been almost fifteen years since I watched the film *Titanic,* and I'm still trying to recover from seeing Kate Winslet topless. The scene probably lasted less than ten seconds, but five thousand days and nights later it's still in my scrapbook. I can't get rid of it. Thankfully the image is finally beginning to fade.

If your husband was sexually active before he married you, his scrapbook may contain material from his previous lovers. While some men actively hold on to these memories, most would love to erase them. But the male brain is not a hard drive. It cannot be reformatted. The persistence of sexual memories is one of the chief reasons pornography and pre-marital sex are so dangerous. Scrapbook images can intrude uninvited on a couple's sex life (as when a husband imagines himself with another woman while making love to his wife, or he can't get an erection without looking at an X-rated video). This is a source of much dysfunction in many marriages.

Ironically, many women make the situation worse without even realizing it. Do you leave magazines like *Cosmopolitan* or *Shape* lying on the coffee table? Do you subscribe to the Victoria's Secret catalog? Do you watch trashy TV shows with half-naked women prancing across the screen? Get these out of your house. Make your home a temptation-free zone for your husband.

So this is what *Men are visual* means. We're excited by what we see. We retain what we see. We are affected for years by what we see.

It comforts me to know that Jesus Christ experienced every temptation common to man yet he did not sin (Hebrews 4:15). This verse means Christ must have been tempted sexually. Christ had a scrapbook. I can think of three instances when the temptation would have been almost unbearable.

In John 4, Jesus is on a business trip. He's in Samaria, a place where he's unknown. He's tired, hungry, and thirsty. He asks a foreign woman for a drink. She's probably very attractive, having snared five men as previous husbands and now living with a sixth. The disciples were away buying bread. It would have been very easy for Jesus to take advantage of the situation—out of town, away from everyone he knew, with a woman who'd bedded at least half-a-dozen men. Yet he did not sin.

The second instance took place in the temple (John 8). The Pharisees brought to Jesus a woman caught in adultery and asked him if she should be stoned according to the law of Moses. Christ simply knelt and wrote in the sand and then uttered the famous words: "Let him who is without sin among you be the first to throw a stone at her" (v. 7 ESV). One by one the men left. Think of the power Jesus had over this woman—he had just saved her life. Her gratitude would have been overwhelming. She was an adulteress—and they were alone. Yet he did not sin.

In Luke 7, a "sinful" woman (probably a prostitute) came to Jesus weeping. She spent a good long time caressing and kissing his feet, anointing them with oil and tears, and wiping them with her own hair. Now, if a prostitute did that to me, I'm not sure what would be going through my head, but it probably wouldn't be the Psalms. Yet he did not sin.

Jesus was tempted sexually yet he did not sin. Sexual thoughts must have run through his mind—yet he mastered them. Temptation is not sin. It's what we do with temptation that matters.

You need to understand that your husband is under a constant barrage of sexual temptation. If he peeks at another woman now and then, don't freak out. (In fact, if he doesn't find a twenty-year-old woman in a bikini attractive, you've got a much bigger problem on your hands.)

I'm not saying, "Oh, just let him look." I'm saying, "If he does look, don't file for divorce." If your husband has stayed faithful to you while immersed in the most tempting society in human history, he does not deserve your condemnation—he deserves a medal.

Chapter 15 is full of ideas on how you can help your husband win this battle. But I'll give you one little piece of advice now: The next time you catch your husband stealing a glance at that twenty-year-old in the bikini, don't think to yourself, *I'm so ugly. He doesn't find me attractive anymore.* Instead, tell yourself, *Provider is calling to him.* Then wrap your arms around him and say, "I know you're tempted all the time, and I just want you to know how much I appreciate your faithfulness to me."

And if you really want to delete that bikini from his scrapbook, tell him what you're going to do with him when you get him alone.

PART THREE

UNDERSTANDING YOUR HUSBAND'S SOUL

Now we examine the soul of a man, the second element of his tripartite nature: body, soul, and spirit.

We all understand what the body is, but what's the difference between soul and spirit? According to the New Testament, they are not the same thing:

For the word of God is living and powerful, and sharper than any two-edged sword, piercing even to *the division of soul and spirit,* and of joints and marrow, and is a discerner of the thoughts and intents of the heart. (Hebrews 4:12 NKJV, emphasis mine)

The soul is often described as "the seat of emotions and desires," whereas the spirit is "the seat of God." Our soul is the sum of our consciousness. It can interact with God, but is not in direct communion with God, as our spirit is.

Confused? It gets worse. Many theologians divide the soul into yet another trinity: mind, will, and emotions. They base their theory on a number of Scripture passages (too many to go into here). They also point out that Christ's inner circle had three men who represented this trinity: James, the mind; Peter, the will; and John, the emotions.

Over the next four chapters, I'll be opening a window into your man's mind, will, and emotions—and what he isn't telling you about each one.

8

His Soul's Greatest Need

There's a disquieting scene in the film *Courageous*. Adam Mitchell and his nine-year-old daughter, Emily, are waiting outside a bank while a friend deposits a check. One of Emily's favorite songs pops onto the radio. She jumps out of the vehicle and invites her daddy to come dance with her. Adam refuses. She asks again and again, even showing him how. But he just can't bring himself to dance with his daughter.

What was Adam afraid of? Why are so many men like this?

The greatest need of a man's soul is to be found competent. Your husband needs to be skilled at something. And his skill needs to be recognized by others.

On the flip side, men harbor a deep fear of incompetence. There is nothing more paralyzing to a man than the prospect of being found deficient, unskilled, or clumsy at a particular task. Dr. John Gray writes in *Men Are from Mars, Women Are from Venus*:

A man's deepest fear is that he is not good enough or that he is incompetent. He compensates for this fear by focusing on increasing his power and competence. Success, achievement, and efficiency are foremost in his life.[1]

Adam Mitchell refused to dance with his daughter because he was afraid of looking foolish in public. He knew what was right, but he just couldn't bring himself to do it.

Fear of incompetence causes a man to gravitate toward the things he is good at, while avoiding anything he's not. Bill and Pam Farrel write:

> A man will strategically organize his life in boxes and then spend most of his time in the boxes in which he can succeed. Success is such a strong motivation for him that he will seek out boxes that work and ignore boxes that confuse him or make him feel like a failure.[2]

That's pretty much all you need to know about your husband's soul in a single paragraph. He will naturally seek experiences that make him feel skilled, while avoiding ones that have the potential to make him feel foolish.

When I was twenty-two I got my first career-track job. My boss was an avid golfer, so he encouraged me to take up the sport—until he saw me play. We both quickly realized I had absolutely no knack for golf. Incompetence doesn't describe it. So after a few rounds I did what men do—I put away my clubs and never touched them again.

If a man can't win, he doesn't want to play.

Your husband's need to be competent can become a source of frustration for you. Let's say your husband decides to remodel a bathroom. A year later all he's done is pull down the old wallpaper and poke a few holes in the Sheetrock. The bathroom looks terrible and you can't seem to get him to move forward on the project.

You might think hubby is lazy, but in reality he may be afraid to dive in because he's feeling incompetent. He's put himself in a tough spot—he said he could do the job but now he's having second thoughts. Consider his options:

1. Start the job and make his incompetence obvious to all
2. Ask for help from a friend, admitting he needs assistance
3. Concede that the task is beyond him and hire a professional
4. Ignore the bathroom and do other things he's good at

What do most men do in this situation? Number four. They avoid the "remodel bathroom" box and spend their time playing with the boxes they feel confident in. Work. Hobbies. Entertainment. By never even attempting a job at which he might fail, your husband protects himself from being found incompetent. It's Protector at work again, shielding your husband from the embarrassment he'd face if the truth were known.

Back to the subject of dancing: I know lots of married women who love to dance, but their husbands absolutely refuse to shake a leg. Wives try to coax their husbands onto the floor, but it's like trying to move a mountain range. Eventually these women end up dancing with other women or sometimes other men. Even a husband's jealousy at seeing his betrothed in the arms of a rival is not enough to make him overcome his fear of being seen as incompetent.

Men are happiest:

• When they are doing something they are good at
• When they can provide for themselves and their families without assistance from others
• When they can figure out something by themselves

- When they are performing at a high level
- When their accomplishments are recognized
- When they are the best at something
- When they can navigate without asking for directions (but you knew that, didn't you?)

Men never forget their triumphs and failures. Here are two of mine, from the year 1971. I was a fifth grader with strong legs and weak arms. That made me a very good kickball player, but I simply could not do the monkey bars. I'd lose my grip and fall after the third or fourth rung. I was deeply embarrassed by this, so I naturally avoided the bars.

One day I was horrified to learn that the monkey bars were a part of the Field Day fitness assessment. I was going to have to perform the monkey bars in front of the entire class! I can remember being worried sick for about two weeks leading up to Field Day. I knew I was going to fail—and sure enough I did. I endured taunting from the other boys in the class for flunking my fitness test. It stung.

But kickball was a different story. Our class had won the fifth grade kickball championship, and I was one of the best players on our team. We were set to play the sixth graders for the school trophy. The older kids had never played against us. They had no idea which players were strong kickers—so I hatched a plan to take advantage of the situation.

When it was my turn to kick, the bases were loaded. As a ruse, I weakly fouled off my first two kicks. My teammates, who were in on the ploy, shouted encouragement. "C'mon David, you can do it!" The outfielders began creeping in, convinced I'd be an easy out. On the third kick, I boomed the ball over their heads deep into left field. Four runs scored, and we eventually beat the sixth graders, thanks to that grand slam.

Talk about a competence shot! Needless to say, I felt pretty good about myself for weeks. I had used my physical strength and my wits to defeat a superior enemy. That's about as manly as it gets.

It's been forty years since I was a fifth grader. But here is the truth: Even as I recounted these two stories, I felt shame about my failure on the monkey bars, but I gloried in telling you about the kickball game. Four decades later one still hurts but the other makes me feel good all over.

Here's something your husband hasn't told you: He faced his own set of monkey bars as a kid. There was a mountain he just couldn't climb. Maybe a lot of mountains. He may have been teased or bullied when he failed to perform. And those wounds still hurt today.

After each little episode of incompetence, Protector came alongside him and locked up part of his heart so it could never be hurt again.

Your husband still faces monkey bars today—but very few men have the courage to ask for help. It's considered unmanly. Most men would rather bumble their way through a challenge than ask for assistance.

One August day I was out on an oil-drilling platform in the Arctic Ocean. A tugboat had pulled alongside and was offloading supplies to the rig. Deckhands secured the loads in a sling and then a crane lifted the cargo up onto the platform, where the drillers loosened the sling and sent it back down for the next load.

The operation ran smoothly until the deckhands had a bit of trouble getting the sling under a bulky pump. It took about fifteen minutes for them to figure out how to lift it. As the deckhands tried various rigging methods, the drillers on the platform laughed uncontrollably. They uttered various curses and epithets under their breath to describe the men's incompetence. Because the deckhands had not mastered the task immediately, the drillers dismissed them as idiots.

Pointing out weakness and incompetence in another man is a time-honored way that men feel good about themselves. When a man bullies another he feels a sense of superiority, which makes him seem more competent by comparison. *I'm better than that fool,* they think to themselves.

Boys learn that bullies pounce on any vulnerability or weakness. Being competent (and hiding your weaknesses) is a way to survive in school. If you don't mess up, the bullies are more likely to leave you alone. Men carry this survival strategy into adulthood.

Men have many other ways of proving their competence. Young men deny themselves food, sleep, and the other basics of life to prove how tough they are. Before the advent of labor unions, employers used to take advantage of this tendency in men. Bosses worked their employees mercilessly and made fun of fellows who sought lunch and coffee breaks. "What do you mean you're hungry? Get back onto the floor, you lazy, good-for-nothing sissy!" This teasing was more effective than a whip; no man wanted his competence and manhood questioned. Some men literally worked themselves to death.

Men learn early in their careers never to admit they might not be able to do something. Example: Calvin's boss approaches him with a project that's somewhat beyond his skill and expertise. Calvin knows this. But when the boss says, "Can you pull this off?" what does Calvin say? "Sure, boss, I can do that!" The words tumble from his lips before he realizes what he's said. Soon Calvin finds himself in way over his head. He must be very careful how he asks his male co-workers for help or he'll be seen as incompetent. He can't tell his wife he's in trouble, because he can't admit to her that he's sinking.

Now, raise your hand if you've ever tried to help a toddler put on his jacket. One day he's happy for the assistance.

The next day he suddenly declares, "I can do it myself!" He becomes angry if you try to render even the slightest aid.

Shocking truth: Men are just big toddlers. From the age of two they spend their lives wanting to do everything themselves. When men feel independent, strong, wise, skilled, and autonomous, they are happy.

Even men who are dependent on others don't like to admit they are. One time an elderly gentleman visited me when I worked in the Alaska governor's office. This old-timer was worried the state might cancel the Longevity Bonus program, a $250-per-month welfare payment Alaska makes to some of its seniors. Straight-faced, he said to me, "If I lose my Longevity Bonus, I might have to rely on a government handout to get by."

Where does this need to be competent and self-reliant come from? Provider's voice is certainly part of it. If a man can't put food on the table, it doesn't matter that he's a scratch golfer or an expert guitarist. Providing is the core competency a man must have in place before he can take pleasure in his other abilities.

Our hunter ancestors also provide us with a clue. Hunters had to project an air of strength and confidence to their tribes, even when the hunt was going poorly. Any admission of weakness or the possibility of an unsuccessful hunt might cause the group to panic. Thousands of years of conditioning has taught men to keep bad news to themselves, or as Dr. John Gray puts it, to retreat to their caves to work out their problems alone, without any help.

Society plays along with this little fiction. We expect our leaders never to admit weakness or indecision. You'll never hear the president of the United States declare on national TV, "My fellow Americans, I just don't know what to do about the situation in the Middle East. Any ideas?" A leader who admits even the slightest lack of competence will be quickly cast out of office. Politicians are supposed to have all the answers—instantly. They can't even change their minds, or they're dismissed as *flip-floppers*.

Male archetypes in literature and film may have weaknesses, but they never admit them. Captain Kirk would never turn to Spock and say, "The Klingons have us beat. We're toast." We love James Bond because he's so amazingly competent. No matter the challenge he faces, 007 always knows what to do. Joshua is seen in the Old Testament dismissing the cautious advice of ten spies but accepting the counsel of two risk takers.

Incompetence can be dangerous to a man's career. Business gurus love to talk about failure as the gateway to success. But I've known a number of men who took risks on their jobs that didn't pan out—and they're no longer employed in those jobs. Football coaches can be fired over a single play gone wrong. Many men do not have the confidence and drive to plow through multiple defeats, because failure rocks a man's sense of competence.

A good wife will build her husband's sense of competence. The more competent a man feels the more likely Protector is to put down his sword and open the cage. If your husband knows you will never ridicule him if he fails, he's much more likely to stretch himself. Shoot, he might even dance with you.

9

What Your Husband Is Afraid Of

So what is your husband afraid of?

Nothing, to hear him tell it. Has he ever come to you and said, "Honey, I'm really scared about _____"?

Rare is the man who will confess his fears to anyone. As we learned in the previous chapter, men are not supposed to have them or admit them. Even if a man were willing to talk about his apprehensions, where could he do it? Who would listen?

Furthermore, most men don't even know they are afraid. They have spent so many years building the façade of fearlessness and invulnerability, they've begun to believe it themselves. *I'm A-OK. Thumbs-up. Let's roll!*

The reality is men are bound up in fear. It's a constant low-level threat, like a grizzly bear asleep on the porch. Nothing bad may be happening now, but they can't help but worry that one day the bear will awaken and destroy everything they've built.

In the last chapter, we identified fear of incompetence as the root from which every male anxiety grows. According to Professor Sam Keen, "We (men) most fear engulfment, anything that threatens to rob us of our power and control. Women most fear abandonment, isolation, loss of love."[1]

The reason power and control are so important to us is because without them we cannot fulfill our two Adamic roles. Stripped of our health, our wealth, our mental capacities, and our talents, we cannot be men. We cannot protect. We cannot provide.

July 4, 1939, America was riveted by a farewell speech delivered at Yankee Stadium by Lou Gehrig. Together, Gehrig and Babe Ruth were the most potent one-two punch in baseball history. Gehrig was nicknamed "The Iron Horse" for his endurance, having set the major league record for most consecutive games without a day off. But his storied career was cut short when he was diagnosed with amyotrophic lateral sclerosis, or as it came to be known, Lou Gehrig's disease. It's a neurodegenerative disorder that causes a person's muscles to weaken and atrophy. What makes ALS so horrifying is there is no loss of mental capacity; the patient is fully aware as his body wastes away. It cannot be cured.

Gehrig lived every man's nightmare. Over time he lost the ability to stand, to walk, to use his hands, to chew food, to speak, and eventually to breathe. The man who once swatted home runs like flies lacked the strength to blink his eyes. He went from the pinnacle of power to the depths of powerlessness. Eventually his chest muscles stopped working and he suffocated to death on June 2, 1941, at the age of thirty-seven.

This is a gut-level fear your husband harbors: to end up like Lou Gehrig in one form or another, his powers taken, unable to protect or provide, even for himself.

Stephen Arterburn writes, "Men will always want to see themselves as a Sequoia, not a pine twisted by the elements. They want the words Eliphaz spoke to Job to apply to them: 'You will come to the grave in full vigor, like sheaves gathered in season' (Job 5:26)."[2] This is so true. When I hear of a man becoming disabled or ravaged by disease, a voice in my head says, *Poor guy. I'm glad that'll never happen to me. I'm going out on top.* My rational mind knows this is foolish. I'm just as susceptible to disease as the next man, yet something in my brain blocks out the possibility, as if the very idea is too much to bear.

～

Whereas women fear abandonment, men fear disempowerment. Here are some of the ways a man's core fear manifests itself:

Men fear disease and disability. Men are so afraid of debilitating disease they tend to postpone medical care, according to many studies. In the UK, men use the National Health Service at a lower rate than women. Men refuse to visit the doctor, in part because they're afraid of what a diagnosis could mean. And here's an odd fact: Even though women get skin cancer more often than men, more men die from the disease. This anomaly has a simple explanation: Men are much more reluctant to seek medical care, even when symptoms arise.[3]

Cycling champion Lance Armstrong delayed going to the doctor for months after his testicular cancer symptoms appeared. His reluctance allowed the disease to spread throughout his body—and when he finally sought treatment, it was almost too late. Armstrong is rebranding the fight against cancer to make it more relevant to men. LIVESTRONG is his chosen name, and he's declared himself not a cancer victim but a cancer survivor.

A lot of men would rather die than end up disabled. The idea of becoming dependent on others to feed, bathe, and dress them is a keen form of torture. Men fear losing their minds to Alzheimer's disease. They fear colon cancer, having to wear a colostomy bag the rest of their lives. Diabetes means regular dialysis, and emphysema means loss of breath and mobility. I personally know two men who have taken their own lives rather than allow a degenerative disease like ALS or Parkinson's to take it from them.

Apparently, men are even reluctant to admit they have normal aches and pains. British men miss an average of 140 workdays over the course of their careers, compared with 189 days for women, even though women's careers tend to be shorter.[4] Females are found to report much more pain than males, according to a study from Stanford University.[5] Is this because women have a lower pain threshold, or are men simply afraid to admit how much they hurt?

Men fear being unable to provide for loved ones. As we learned in part 2 of this book, basics such as food, clothing, and shelter have been scarce for much of human history. They still are in many areas of the globe. Famine has always been common and unpredictable. As a result, men have learned to worry about providing.

In prehistoric times, hunters had no way to plan for the future. Money had not been invented, so there was no way to sock away wealth for the future. The only currency was food, and that was perishable. In agricultural societies your children were your retirement plan. But in modern society, we must earn a second income for retirement savings. As life expectancy expands, the amount one needs to retire grows ever greater.

This is another new burden on men. It can be a heavy load and a source of real anxiety for your husband. Many Americans believe Social Security is going broke, and a spate of recent articles in business magazines claim that even a million dollars in the bank is not enough to retire on these days. Yikes.

Kiplinger's Personal Finance Magazine listed thirteen scary financial scenarios. Number one was, "Not saving enough for retirement," and number two was, "Outliving your retirement savings."[6] Stephen Arterburn conducted a national survey of 3,600 men. Their number-one point of agreement was this: Men are fearful about financial security now and in retirement.[7]

As a man, Jesus' words are a comfort to me: "Therefore I say to you, do not worry about your life, what you will eat or what you will drink; nor about your body, what you will put on. Is not life more than food and the body more than clothing?" (Matthew 6:25 NKJV). I cling to this verse when I'm tempted to worry about providing adequately for my brood.

Men fear they won't succeed. Americans are supposed to "succeed," whatever that means. We are expected to achieve the American Dream. Men are primarily responsible for making this happen. Provider constantly reminds men of their obligation to be successful and prosperous.

Many men labor under the crushing expectations of parents. I have a friend (let's call him Barry) whose father once said to him, "If you don't go to college, you'll never make anything of yourself." Well, Barry didn't go to college—and he's made something of himself, but at a terrible cost. For years he was a compulsive workaholic, regularly putting in 80- to 100-hour workweeks—and boasting about it. His health and family have suffered. Happily he's found Christ in recent years and reexamined his priorities. Things are getting better for Barry. He's even talking about early retirement.

But for every Barry there are dozens of other men who get trapped in the rat race and never escape—working as hard as they can whether they really need to or not. The good things in life are expensive, and society expects men to provide them.

Rapper 50 Cent named his breakout album *Get Rich or Die Tryin'*. To some men, life isn't worth living if you're not wealthy. In some social circles a man's standing depends on his ability to acquire riches and flaunt them. These men are under enormous pressure to acquire fancy cars, luxurious homes, flashy jewelry, and fabulous vacations.

The "a real man is wealthy" expectation even reaches into certain churches and denominations, where prosperity-preaching pastors are supposed to drive luxury vehicles and dress in expensive suits. I've spoken to ministers who say, "My flock won't follow a poor preacher. If I don't look prosperous, they won't believe God is blessing me and my ministry."

Some men hear Provider's voice so strongly they become greedy. They turn to crime to become wealthy. They become obsessed with wealth building. Or they get taken in by a con man with a get-rich-quick scheme.

Men fear falling behind and losing their edge. For millennia, men's work skills didn't change during their lifetimes. They had one job and they did it until the day they died. Hunters hunted until they were too old to hunt. Farmers farmed until they were too old to farm. But in today's rapidly changing economy, men can become occupationally obsolete in a matter of weeks. Companies go from industry leaders to also-rans almost instantly. Organizations are sold, downsized, and reengineered all the time.

I remember getting a visit from an encyclopedia salesman back in the mid-1990s. He was a big guy, whose suit jacket stretched unwillingly across his barrel chest. He gave us a twenty-minute pitch about the importance of kids having an encyclopedia in the home. When he was done, I turned to the personal computer sitting behind me. "You see that?" I asked him. "In a few years I'll be able to connect it to a vast library of information, hundreds of times more efficient than a paperbound encyclopedia. I'll be able to type in a word or two and dozens of scholarly articles will pop up on the screen in just a few seconds." The salesman closed his briefcase, shook my hand, and walked out the door. We both knew the truth: He'd better look for another job.

Some men are so afraid of falling behind their competitors they risk everything to succeed—including their health. Lyle Alzado was one of the most feared defensive linemen of his era. He was the first NFL player to admit using steroids, which are widely believed to have led to his death at age forty-three. Shortly before he died, Alzado wrote:

> I started taking anabolic steroids in 1969, and I never stopped. . . . Now I'm sick. And I'm scared. . . . I wobble when I walk and sometimes have to hold on to someone for support. You have to give me time to answer questions, because I have trouble remembering things. . . . Ninety percent of the athletes I know are on the stuff. We're not born to be 280 or 300 pounds or jump 30 feet. . . . All along I was taking steroids, and I saw they made me play better and better. I kept on because I knew I had to keep on getting more size. I became very violent on the field. Off it too. I did things only crazy people do.[8]

Men fear being taken away. Men harbor a fear of someday being jailed without cause. Men are still falsely accused and imprisoned every day, particularly in the third world. In some nations, you can be taken away for owning a Bible, for speaking out against the government, or for failing to pay protection money to the local mafia or police force.

American men don't worry about this on a daily basis, but it has crossed our minds. We wonder what we might do if we were locked up or tortured. Would we bear up under suffering, or would we crack under the pressure?

Men fear being publicly embarrassed. A lot of guys would rather jump off a cliff than be embarrassed in front of others. In preindustrial Japan, a Samurai warrior who was defeated committed hari-kari (ritual suicide) rather than live with his disgrace. An athlete's stellar career can be wiped out by a single blunder in a critical game (just go to the Internet and look up Bill Buckner).

And here's something your husband hasn't told you, or maybe he has: He HATES it when you embarrass him in public. If you tease or ridicule your spouse in front of others, you are committing hari-kari in your marriage. DO NOT—I repeat—do not ridicule your husband—either to his face or behind his back. Your husband needs and deserves your unwavering respect.

Men fear being thought of as unmanly. Men do things that affirm their masculinity, while avoiding behaviors that are perceived as womanly by their peers.

Here's the scene: My wife and I are standing in a department store. She's looking at dresses. She turns to me and says, "Honey, hold my purse for a minute." I'm mortified. I don't want to be seen in public holding a purse, because men do not hold purses.

Women can't understand this fear because they actually like manly stuff. If I'm working on the roof and say to my beloved, "Honey, hold my hammer for a minute," she feels no shame. In our society women are free to do manly things, but men are prohibited from doing womanly things.

Here's David Murrow's Iron-Clad Rule of the Genders: Women do masculine, but men don't do feminine. This is why women go to football games, but men don't go to baby showers. Why women wear pants, but men don't wear skirts.

Why women are flooding into so-called men's jobs (doctor, lawyer, and construction worker), but men tend to avoid so-called women's jobs (elementary school teacher, nurse, and office assistant).

Miller beer has launched a multimillion-dollar ad campaign that mocks men who do feminine things, such as going to the bathroom in pairs, wearing skinny jeans, or carrying bags that look like purses. Each ad finishes with a gravel-voiced announcer telling men to "man up" by choosing the beer for men—Miller Lite. By playing on men's fears of being seen as unmanly, they convince men to spend millions on their product.

Men fear losing their families. This is a growing fear among men. I'll reveal why in our next chapter.

10

The Power Women Have Over Men

Popular myth says women have been powerless for centuries and have only recently been liberated from male oppression. On one level this is true: Women have been denied access to the levers of societal power, or "hard power" as some call it. But women have always possessed "soft power." This indirect power is embodied in well-known female archetypes: the Jewish mother who controls her family through guilt, the trophy wife who uses her looks to control a man and his money, the TV housewife who tricks her husband into doing what she wants. As Mama Maria said in the film *My Big Fat Greek Wedding*: "The man is the head [of the house], but the woman is the neck. And she can turn the head any way she wants."

You have much more power over your husband than you may think. Men may rule the wider world, but women rule the sphere that really counts. You have the power to make a man's domestic existence heavenly or hellish. Proverbs 25:24 (NKJV) says, "It is better to dwell in a corner of a housetop, than in a house shared with a contentious woman."

This chapter is about the power distribution in your marriage. How you exercise power in your relationship has a huge bearing on what kind of husband—and marriage—you will have.

Here's something your husband isn't telling you: He lives to please you. Making you happy is one of his greatest joys.

It started in the garden. Eve plucked the fruit. She handed it to her husband. He knew it was wrong, but he ate it anyway. I suppose he was just doing what husbands do—trying to please his wife. I can relate to Adam's predicament. When my wife places food in front of me, I've learned to eat it—and like it, without question and with enthusiasm.

In all honesty, I have never met a man who did not want to please his wife at some level. Your husband may be a self-absorbed cad who has no idea what your "love language" is, but he does want to please you. He may not be very successful at it, but that doesn't mean he's not interested.

Men learn to please women at an early age. The first face a young man sees is that of his mother, staring down at him in pure adoration as he nurses at her breast. At first her smiles come unconditionally. But if he does something that displeases her (like biting down), the boy quickly learns the terror of her wrath. He gets flicked on the cheek or even spanked on the bottom. He begins to learn, "If Mama ain't happy, ain't nobody happy."

Soon the boy realizes he can light up a woman's face by bringing her a flower, eating all his food, or sharing crayons with his sister. In fact, little boys must learn to please

112

a gauntlet of female caregivers—grandmothers, childcare workers, elementary teachers, Sunday school teachers. By the time a boy reaches adolescence, he knows what delights a woman—as well as what terrorizes her.

So here's what your husband isn't telling you: You hold tremendous power over him. No one else can take him to the pinnacle of ecstasy or the depths of despair the way you can. A few words from your mouth can catapult him or crush him. Your face is a mirror that tells him how he's performing as a man.

Here are some ideas to help you use your power wisely.

Learn to use soft power. Women of previous generations were Steel Magnolias—gentle on the outside but durable on the inside. They understood indirect (soft) power, and used it to get what they believed was best for their families.

Like any form of power, soft power has its negative methods, such as guilt, manipulation, and conniving. But it also has its positive methods: gentle persuasion, negotiation, and submission. (That's right—submission is one of the best ways to gain power in your marriage. In God's economy, you gain power by giving it up.)

Soft power is gentle but firm. It's respectful. It's persistent. It's a pleasant breeze—not a raging tornado.

Many of today's women seem to have forgotten about soft power, told by the intelligentsia that the only power worth having is that which men have traditionally wielded. After all, who wants to be the neck when you can be the head?

Counselors are seeing more couples in which both partners are grasping for hard power. This upsets the balance of marriage. Spouses bash away at each other with hard power, while no one exercises the soft power that's so crucial to a successful relationship.

When a woman uses hard power with her husband, he instinctively protects himself. Psychologically he becomes a toddler once again, controlled by a woman who is angry with him. And so he reacts like a toddler—digging in his heels, hiding in his room, or saying, "You're not the boss of me!" Slowly the man disappears and Protector takes his place.

Take an honest look at the kind of power you exert in your marriage. Do you fight dirty with your husband? Do you curse? Throw things? Call him names? Hit below the belt (figuratively or literally)? Belittle him? Try to win an argument at all costs? If you do these things to your man, I fear you will not be married long. If you want to preserve your marriage, you must be respectful toward your husband, even in the midst of conflict.

Learning to cleverly use soft power will not only get you what you want, it will make your husband happy to give it to you. I offer some advice on how to exert soft power in chapter 16.

Use your economic power wisely. Men still out-earn women, but the income gap is closing. Young, single, childless women now out-earn their male counterparts.[1] This is one reason why women eighteen to thirty-four are the most sought-after audience for advertisers—they make most of the purchasing decisions and control the expendable income. With more women than men earning advanced degrees and employed in the workforce, expect this to continue.

Meanwhile, men's economic power is declining. Blue-collar "men's jobs" are being destroyed by the millions, while pink-collar "women's jobs" are expanding. The Great Recession that began in 2007 has been dubbed the "he-cession," because about 75 percent of the job losses fell on men. In 1950, 5 percent of U.S. men at the prime working age were jobless. In 2010, the number was 20 percent.[2] And in 2010, for the first time, more women were employed in the workforce than men.

Adding to men's stress is the fact that many wives now out-provide their husbands. Men who are married to "breadwinner wives" often lose respect for themselves, causing their wives to lose respect for them. Men feel terrible when they can't pick up the check at restaurants or have to ask their wives for money. Sex dries up. Divorce often follows.[3]

If you out-earn your husband, you need to realize how emasculating this situation can be. Do whatever you can to preserve his pride. If he wants to pay for dinner, by all means let him. Then thank him—even if the money originally came from your paycheck.

Use your power within the family wisely. Some women take total control of their children's discipline, education, and activities, leaving their husbands with little input. As a result, some men feel shut out of their children's lives.

Society is magnifying this trend. Masculine ways of child rearing are "out" while feminine ones are "in":

What's "out"	What's "in"
Spanking	Verbal discipline
Keeping score	Everyone gets a trophy
"You failed"	"Nice try!"
Self-discipline	Self-esteem
Free play	Playdates
"You're not hurt, get up and play"	"Oh, you poor baby!"
Independent young adults	Helicopter parenting
Winners and losers	"Everyone's special!"

One beautiful summer afternoon I was on the playground with my four-year-old grandson. He got into a little tussle with another boy over the last remaining kiddie swing. Seated on a bench to my right were the parents of the other boy. Mom spotted the altercation and began to rise to her feet.

Her husband gently touched her arm and said, "Honey, let them work it out." The boys kept tugging. She shot an exasperated look at her spouse and then sprang into action. Seconds later she was mediating the dispute. I looked at the other dad. He looked at me. We shook our heads.

Ladies, sometimes Father does know best—even when you may think he doesn't. A mom is like a she-bear: Her only goal is to protect and comfort her cubs *right now*. But fathers tend to see the bigger picture. Men understand that conflict is inevitable in life, and the playground is a great place for kids to learn the art of negotiation.

Here's something your husband isn't telling you: He's happy to cede the majority of family responsibility to you—but he wants to give input. Many men feel they have something valuable to offer, but their ways are being vilified by the larger society. You need to honor your husband's approach to child rearing, particularly when it comes to discipline, even if his methods seem tough or harsh. Let Dad be Dad—unless he clearly crosses the line into abuse or neglect.

Use your turf power wisely. Education is my wife's area of expertise. She's worked in the public schools for years. She homeschooled two of our three kids. I pretty much let her run this show—but I still want to give input.

One time my wife and youngest daughter were planning out the courses she would be taking in the fall. I overheard their conversation, and something didn't sound right. So I asked them, "Are you sure that course applies to her graduation requirements?" They shot each other a quick glance, as if to say, "The village idiot has spoken again." My wife looked at me, and with a slightly condescending tone proceeded to give me a terse explanation of the course and why it counted. It still sounded like a waste of time to me, but I backed off because I felt unqualified to comment any further.

The bigger issue here was how my wife was using her turf power. She made me feel like an intruder, and my input was not welcome. "Out of my kitchen," she was saying, figuratively. "You are incompetent here."

This plays into one of men's greatest insecurities: the feeling of being inadequate as a dad. Here's something your husband isn't telling you: At work he's a genius, but at home he's a dunce.

I have a friend who's probably one of the best auto mechanics in Alaska. He can often tell you what's wrong with a car just by listening to it. He's well respected around town for his skill as a grease monkey. But the moment he steps through the front door of his home, he becomes an idiot. His teenage daughter thinks he's a simpleton. His wife doesn't trust his judgment on anything. He knows how to deal with balky starter solenoid, but has no idea how to manage a snippy teenage girl.

This is a big reason men pour their energies into work but not their families. They are competent at work. They're trained and certified. But at home they are amateurs.

If you want your husband to be more involved with the family, be very careful about shooing him away. Invite him onto your turf. Ask his advice. Let him know his point of view is valued, even when he offers it unexpectedly. He'll be more involved and less isolated. If you make him feel incompetent in the domestic sphere, he'll eventually give up and cede it to you.

Use your sexual power wisely. You alone have the power to transport your husband to the stars. Here's a little parable to help you understand why it's so important to take him there regularly.

Let's say you're a chocoholic. All day long you see advertisements for chocolate. You see people eating chocolate. You fantasize about sinking your teeth into a raspberry hazelnut praline or an Italian espresso truffle. You think, *Right after work I'm going to my favorite chocolate shop and indulge my fantasy.* But when you arrive, the shop is closed. Again.

When it comes to chocolate, if one store is closed, you can go to another one. But your husband has just one place to go for his favorite thing. If the store is consistently closed, what message are you sending him? *Get your ya-yas somewhere else, buddy.* Months later you're shocked to find your husband engaged in masturbation, porn, or an extramarital affair.

Here's something your husband isn't telling you: He needs you to be generous with the chocolate. He understands that some days the store just can't be open. But your regular, enthusiastic lovemaking is vital to his mental well-being. It's his greatest joy, and he has nowhere else to go for it. And you want to keep it that way.

Wives who consistently refuse sex to their husbands (or who use sex as a reward for good behavior) are asking for trouble. The apostle Paul says, "The husband should fulfill his marital duty to his wife, and likewise the wife to her husband. The wife does not have authority over her own body but yields it to her husband. In the same way, the husband does not have authority over his own body but yields it to his wife. Do not deprive each other except perhaps by mutual consent and for a time, so that you may devote yourselves to prayer. Then come together again so that Satan will not tempt you because of your lack of self-control."[4]

A woman who regularly deprives her husband, puts conditions on sex, or makes her husband feel as if she's doing him a favor by making love to him is eroding the very foundation of her marriage.

Use divorce power wisely. For thousands of years, men held all the power in marriage. If a man divorced his wife, she and the children were likely to starve. Even today, we hear horror stories of "starter wives" who worked two jobs to put their husbands through law school, only to be dumped for younger "trophy wives" once these men became successful. And it's still true that divorce pushes many women into poverty.[5]

But in the past thirty years, divorce power has swung in the other direction. This is the trump card you hold over your husband. You have the power to take his family away from him.

Women initiate two-thirds of all divorces today. States with no-fault divorce see 70 percent of cases filed by women, and among college-educated couples, the figure increases to 90 percent.[6] The more financially independent the woman, the more likely she is to bail on her marriage.

A lot of women are walking away from marriages that probably could have been saved. A study of 46,000 divorces in four states found that just "6 percent were granted on grounds of violence, and husbands were cited for adultery only slightly more often than wives." Dr. Margaret F. Brining, a law professor at the University of Iowa notes, "Some women file for divorce because they're exploited in really bad marriages. But it seems to be a relatively small number, probably less than 20 percent of the cases."

And why do so many women seek divorce? According to Dr. Brining's research, women often see divorce as a way of gaining more control over their kids: "Children are the most important asset in a marriage, and the partner who expects to get sole custody is by far the most likely to file for divorce."[7] Women are granted custody of their children more than 80 percent of the time, according to figures from the U.S. Census.[8] Women have little to fear from divorce because they know they'll get the kids. Seventy-nine percent of men agreed with this statement: Men get screwed by the courts in divorce.[9] (Forty-one percent of women agreed as well.)

This has led to what some call the *Eat, Pray, Love* syndrome (named after the story line of the popular book and movie): empowered women walking away from acceptable unions because they feel unfulfilled, they're disappointed in their husbands, or they've met another man they'd rather be with. Some American women are practicing hypergamy, or "marrying up" to successively wealthier men. I personally know two women who divorced and remarried into a higher income bracket. When I met "Olivia," she lived in a shabby trailer shortly after her first marriage; today she inhabits a 4,000-square-foot home in an exclusive neighborhood, courtesy of her wealthy third husband.

For a woman, a divorce means a loss of income, but for the man it often means the loss of his family, his home, and his possessions. Many times the divorced husband must watch as another man takes his place at the family dinner table and in the marriage bed. Women who want to play dirty can accuse their husbands of emotional or even physical abuse (with little corroborating evidence). If the judge believes her, the husband never sees his children again.

I've talked to a lot of men who were completely blindsided when their wives asked for a divorce. "I thought everything was fine, and she just walks in one day and says she's leaving," said Lenny, a thirty-year-old computer programmer from Dallas. "The only reason she gave is I'm not meeting her needs, whatever that means."

Why are so many men surprised when their wives ask for a divorce? Because most men are happy with their marriages—and they think their wives are too.

Here's something your husband isn't telling you: Men compare marriages. Here's how they think: *Hey, my marriage isn't perfect, but it's a lot better than most. It's better than my parents' marriage. And it's way better than the marriages on TV. So I guess we're doing okay.*

In general, women bring higher expectations into marriage than men do. Women start planning their weddings at age five. Their earliest role models are the Disney princesses, all of whom find their beasts, change them into handsome princes, marry them, and live happily ever after. Expectations ratchet higher as teenage girls consume a steady diet of romance novels and romantic comedy films. Young women immerse themselves in celebrity relationships through gossip magazines. So by the time a woman arrives at the altar she's already spent twenty years or more imagining exactly how married life is going to be. Men, on the other hand, rarely do much thinking about marriage until they meet a girl they get serious about.

Because men bring only scant expectations to marriage, they tend to be satisfied with what they get. A whopping 95 percent of men would marry their spouse again (compared to 85 percent of women).[10] Some women set their expectations so high they are inevitably disappointed when their husband turns out to be Shrek instead of Prince Charming.

I'm not saying divorce is always wrong. Even Christ made an exception for adultery. If your husband is physically abusing you or the kids, you need to get away.

But some women use the prospect of a divorce, a custody battle, and a costly settlement as a cudgel to keep their men in line. Threat of divorce is the golden ring of power in your marriage. The more you put it on your finger, the more you become like Gollum, the crooked character from the Lord of the Rings trilogy.

I like the title of Dr. Christine Meinecke's book *Everybody Marries the Wrong Person*. The same temptation that's snared foolish men for centuries is now capturing a generation of newly empowered women. Too often women give up on a salvageable union because they think they married Mr. Wrong. They say to themselves, "This is such an awful relationship. It can't be God's will. If I try again, I might find the one God has for me."

Reality check: According to Scripture, the man you are married to *is* the man God has for you. Remember, over 90 percent of the marriages in human history have been arranged by parents and matchmakers. Marriage came first—love came later. Yet it did come. If you feel trapped in a loveless marriage, you're in good company. Never forget: With God, all things are possible.

11

Why He Won't Share His Feelings

Author Warren Farrell tells the story of Ralph, a junior partner in a law firm who worked long hours to provide for his family. He thought he was being noble, sacrificing his own dreams so his wife could have a nice home and his kids could afford a top-notch education.

One day he came home with some great news—after years of toil, he had finally made senior partner. But his wife was not pleased. She accused him of being a workaholic, and ordered him to attend a men's support group—or she would leave him.

So Ralph went. For three months he never said a word in the group. Then one day he finally told his story. "I feel like I've spent forty years, working as hard as I could, to become somebody I don't even like," he said. "I've lost my family, I've lost my wife, and I've lost myself." For the first time in decades, Ralph broke down and cried. He got lots of care and affirmation from the men in his group. He began realizing that he'd been listening too closely to Provider, and his confession was the first tentative step he made toward the headwaters of his soul.

But a few days later Ralph made a devastating mistake. "I was mentioning some of my doubts to a few of my associates at work," Ralph said. "They listened attentively for a couple of minutes, then one made a joke, and another excused himself. Finally I mentioned this men's group—which I never should have done—and they just laughed me out of the office. I've been the butt of their jokes ever since. Suddenly I realized [my wife] has a whole network of lady friends she can talk with . . . yet the men I've worked with for seventeen years, sixty hours a week, hardly know me. Nor do they want to."[1]

There's enormous pressure on men to keep their true feelings bottled up inside. In most social circles, males are allowed to talk about exactly four things—sports, weather, politics, and hobbies. Men can also talk about their families, but only certain topics are permitted—how busy everyone is, their children's sports activities, and how well everything is going.

Men who speak honestly about their challenges or yearnings are ridiculed as "navel gazers" by other men. We certainly can't acknowledge our weaknesses, fears, or pain. We're like the black knight in *Monty Python and the Holy Grail*—arms hacked off, bleeding to death, yet we say to ourselves and others, "It's just a flesh wound. I'm invincible!"

It's easy to blame your husband's silence about his feelings on the expectations of society. But that's not the main reason he won't tell you what he's really thinking. I'm about to reveal one of the most shocking truths your husband isn't telling you.

Most men do not tell their wives what they really feel because if they did, their wives would punish them for it. That's right. When men tell the truth, the whole truth, and nothing but the truth, their wives often become upset. Very upset.

I've spoken to lots of men who decided early in their marriages to open up and speak the absolute truth. And their wives freaked out, withdrew, cried, threw tantrums, and plugged their ears. These men learned very quickly that their wives didn't want to hear the truth—and that the key to marital bliss was to carefully manage what they did and didn't tell their beloved.

Is this hard to hear? Dear reader, I'm just telling you a truth I've heard from the lips of dozens of men. Here are some of their stories (names and details changed to protect identities).

Ernie was a happily married man. He loved his wife dearly. The couple operated a small office furniture business together in a suburb of a large city. They had been married nine years. They had no children except their dogs and cats.

Ernie confided with me that he had been molested as a young teenager, and ever since that tragic event he had struggled with same-sex attraction. Although he had never acted on those urges with another man, he had occasionally used the Internet to access gay porn sites. He felt terrible about his compulsion but hadn't known what to do about it.

Despite these urges, he and his wife enjoyed a satisfying sex life. He found her attractive and interesting. They enjoyed good communication and he was quite satisfied with his marriage. He assumed his wife was happy as well.

One Sunday he heard a sermon about confession. The pastor used James 5:16 as his text: "Therefore confess your sins to each other and pray for each other so that you may be healed."

Ernie had a God moment. His wife knew about the molestation, but he'd never confessed his temptations or his struggles with porn. He knew what he had to do. As soon as he and his wife got home from church he sat her down on the couch and told her everything.

As soon as she heard the words "gay porn," she burst into tears and ran screaming out of the room, literally sticking her fingers in her ears so she would hear no more. She got in her car and drove to her parents' house. She did not return. She refused to answer his calls. She completely froze him out.

A few days later Ernie got a phone call from one of the elders in the church, inviting him for coffee. All the way to Starbucks his stomach was in knots. *Maybe I should tell the elder my wife and I have separated so he can pray for us,* Ernie thought.

Turned out Ernie didn't need to say a thing. The elder already knew the truth—and more. Apparently Ernie's wife had told a church friend what had happened—in great detail. That friend told another friend, and within hours the story spread like a virus through the church. Fueled by gossip, the account of Ernie's sins had grown. The elder accused Ernie of operating a gay porn site and having been involved in multiple homosexual relationships over the years. Ernie tried to set the record straight, but the elder was in no mood to listen. "I'm not here to hear your confession and mete out penance," the elder said. "I'm here to challenge you about sin in your life. Either you repent or find another church."

Ernie drove to his in-laws' house and confronted his wife. Instead of apologizing for ruining his reputation, she presented him with divorce papers.

Let's stop the story right here. Admittedly, Ernie should have told his wife about his compulsions years ago. It was a lot for her to absorb and she had every right to be upset.

But her reaction was completely inappropriate. Ernie's wife was blinded by her pain. She could not see the good man in front of her trying to do the right thing. Here was a man who truly loved her, telling her the absolute truth. He was looking for help. He believed James 5:16—that if he confessed his sins to his wife she would pray for him and he could be healed. And here's what his confession cost him: his marriage, his church, and eventually his business. He even lost the dogs and cats.

Admittedly this is an extreme example of what can happen to a man who tells his wife the truth. Far more common is a story like this one told by Stephen Arterburn:

> Dan loved his wife and would never be unfaithful to her, but a woman at work had caught his eye. She was beautiful and had showed an interest in him. She would stop by his office to talk—always about safe subjects such as her boyfriend or Dan's wife. But this woman's presence had become a factor in Dan's life. He didn't know what to do, but he managed to narrow his choices down to two: defuse the situation by talking to his wife about it, including her, and seeking her help in resolving his feelings, or keep the situation and his feelings to himself so as not to threaten his wife.
>
> He decided to talk to his wife, to invite her into the situation as an ally. After dinner one night, when the children were in bed and the two of them were alone in the kitchen, he broached the subject as carefully as he knew how. He reaffirmed his love for his wife but told her he wanted her to be aware that there was a woman at work showing interest in him. Trying to be honest, he told his wife she was attractive and that he had been surprised by the fact that he looked forward to their chats.
>
> Up to that point, his wife had been with him. But when he told her how he felt about the woman stopping by his office, she began to cry and ran upstairs to their bedroom. She was inconsolable, and he ended up spending the night on the sofa downstairs. Naturally, he concluded that he had made a gigantic mistake by revealing what was going on at work and, more important, his own feelings about the events. Wishing

he could take the whole conversation back, he decided he would never risk that kind of honesty again.

He kept to his word, and within a month he had slept with the woman at work. It only happened once. But he decided that "once burned, twice shy" was a good reason not to tell his wife.[2]

I have a good friend who became a Christian four years ago. But he still has not told his wife because she sees "organized religion" as oppressive to women. My friend would love to be honest, but over a quarter-century of marriage he's been trained not to do anything that might rile her. A decade ago he had a brief extramarital affair and it's taken him years to win back her trust. "We are finally at a pretty good place," he says. "If I told her the truth about my faith it would just get her upset again." It's sad. My friend is unable to share the most significant thing that ever happened to him because he fears his wife's wrath.

I have another friend who is a pastor. He must be extremely careful what he shares with his wife about the church or she will fall into a tailspin of depression. He cannot tell her his true feelings about his parishioners or she'll absorb his anxiety. He carefully sifts through the events of his day and tells her only those things that are least likely to upset her.

A lot of women have trained their husbands to conceal the truth from them. Put yourself in your husband's shoes. He takes a huge risk to be honest with you. And what is his reward? Silence, anger, crying, hitting, verbal abuse, gossip, depression, or in extreme cases, divorce. The minimum sentence is a night on the sofa. Is it any wonder why men don't tell their wives the truth?

At this point you may be thinking, *I would never do that to my husband.* Okay, take this little quiz. How might you react if your husband told you one of the following:

- He disapproves of one of your friends.
- He's thinking of quitting his steady job to pursue his dream.
- He's unhappy in your church.
- He thinks you should dress differently.
- He's being tempted by another woman.
- He feels unsupported by you.
- He wants you to take a harder line disciplining the kids.
- He thinks you're wearing too much makeup.
- He's feeling a little bored by your sex life and he'd like to try some new things.
- There won't be enough money for the vacation you've been planning.
- He wants to buy a boat.
- He wishes you'd lose weight.
- He feels you're spending too much money.
- He answers, "Yes, that dress *does* make you look fat."

Honestly, what would happen if your husband told you these sorts of things? Would you remain calm? (maybe). Would you smile at him and thank him for being honest? (not likely). Would you haul him into the bedroom and make love to him? (not for at least a week).

You may be wondering why guys are such wimps. Why don't they have the gumption to tell women the truth?

Imagine you're housebreaking a puppy. Every time he soils the rug he gets a swat. But if he does his business outside, you lavish rewards on him. Eventually the dog does what he's trained to do—not because he wants to, but because it's the only way to avoid punishment.

Now, imagine you're training a husband. Every time he tells you the absolute truth he gets a swat. But when he conceals his true feelings, you lavish rewards on him. Eventually he begins carefully managing what he tells you—not because he wants to, but because it's the only way to avoid punishment.

If you penalize your man each time he tells you his true feelings, here's the message you are sending: "If you want your life to be hell, tell me the truth. If you want things to go smoothly, lie to me; tell me only those things that will keep me happy in my delusions."

Now, let me guess what you're thinking. You're either sifting through your memory bank, wondering if you've ever punished your husband for telling the truth. Or you are feeling very angry at me for saying these hurtful things about your gender. In fact, you may be ready to punish me, by dismissing me as a misogynist for even suggesting women could engage in such reprehensible behavior.

Don't misunderstand me: I am not blaming women for every communication glitch in marriage. Husbands do the same things to wives. I know women who can't tell their husbands the truth because they're afraid they'll become angry. Women suffer too. I get it.

The point I'm making is this: I'm simply asking you to open your eyes to the possibility that you are contributing to your husband's silence. Consider that you may have unwittingly trained him to hide his true heart from you.

This brings up another thing your husband isn't telling you: Men are tired of being seen as 100 percent of the problem in their marriages. Dr. Willard Harley Jr. writes:

Each day I am confronted by women who are extremely frustrated with their marriages. They usually express no hope that their husbands will ever understand what it is that frustrates them, let alone change enough to solve the problem. From their perspective, marital problems are created by their husbands who do little or nothing to solve them. Wives tend to see themselves as the major force for resolving conflicts, and when they give up their effort, the marriage is usually over.

When I talk to their husbands, they usually have a very different explanation as to why their wives feel the way they do. They often feel that the expectations of women in general and their wives in particular, have grown completely out of reach. These men, who feel that they've made a gigantic effort to be caring and sensitive to their wives, get no credit whatsoever for their sizeable contribution to the family. They feel under enormous pressure to improve their financial support, improve the way they raise their children, and improve the way they treat their wives. Many men I see are emotionally exhausted and feel that for all their effort, they get nothing but criticism.[3]

I resonate with Dr. Harley's assessment. Twice in our marriage, my wife has sent me to counseling to fix "my issues." Both times the counselor helped us see the problem stemmed as much from my wife's issues as it did from mine. It was only after both of us owned our share of the problem that things got better.

Ironically, many churches unwittingly reinforce the idea that men are flawed. Every Mother's Day churches gush over moms, but on Father's Day the message is "Straighten up, Bub!" Honesty check: When you hear of a couple in your church that is having marital problems, who do you assume is to blame, him or her? I'll admit it—I immediately suspect the husband. The church has trained me to think that men are flawed and in need of repair but women are inherently virtuous.

Easy, widespread divorce is causing generations of boys to grow up fatherless. Worse yet, many boys are being raised by women who made the decision that they were better off without a man. Some of these women are bitter toward their ex-husbands, and their poisoned attitudes may be causing their sons to believe men are dangerous, irresponsible, mean, and unnecessary. This is another reason we see so many young men refusing to grasp opportunities and assert themselves in the world—they've absorbed a message that men are worthless and manly pursuits are suspect. They see it as far safer for everyone if they live small lives and allow women to take the lead.

Men are punished for sharing their true feelings. Punished by their friends. Punished by society. And punished by their wives. Is it any wonder they're so good at concealing them?

You know what to do. The next time your husband shares what's on his heart, no matter how shocking, thank him. Believe in him. Don't dismiss his concerns. Don't become upset with him. No matter what he says, trust that God has the situation under control.

UNDERSTANDING YOUR HUSBAND'S SPIRIT

Quick quiz:

- In your experience, which gender is more "spiritual," males or females?
- In your church, are there more male or female volunteers?
- In your extended family, are there more males or females walking with Jesus?
- In your own marriage, who is more enthusiastic about spiritual pursuits, the male or the female?

Let me guess: You answered *female* to at least three of those questions.

Would it surprise you to learn that throughout human history men have been far more religious than women? Anthropologist Ernestine Friedl found that in almost all hunter-gatherer societies, men were the keepers of religion. This "includes the idea that men are responsible for controlling sacred or spiritual aspects of the universe and women the profane or secular aspects."[1]

As societies moved into agriculture, men still played an outsize role in religion. Our Bible reflects this: It's primarily the story of heroic men serving God. Every major world religion was founded by a man and his male disciples.

But as with everything else, industrialization changed religion remarkably. Modern Christianity has begun morphing into a "woman's thing." While men still control the pulpit, women are dominating the pews. The numbers don't lie: The average U.S. congregation draws an adult crowd that's 61 percent female and 39 percent male. Overseas' congregations report gender gaps as high as ten-to-one. Women's Bible study groups outnumber men's by about three-to-one.[2]

Why have laymen largely relinquished their role as leaders in the church? In the next three chapters, I'll be addressing the mysterious, frustrating spiritual lives of men. If your husband is a follower of Jesus and an enthusiastic churchgoer, these chapters may not have a lot to say to you. But read them anyway. You need to know what he's not telling you—about God, about church, and about the role of faith in your marriage.

12

Why You Like Church Better Than He Does

I know almost nothing about plants, but greenery is my wife's love language. One day I decided to surprise her with a planter, and being a cheapskate, I thought I'd create my own. I went to Walmart and bought a small flowering azalea, some ivy, a decorative pot, and some soil. I put the whole thing together and presented it to her after dinner. She was impressed—for about two weeks. That's when the azalea started looking rather sickly. Its blossoms fell off and its little leaves turned brown. But the ivy was flourishing—same pot, same soil, same light, same water. I was puzzled.

I called a friend who is a master gardener. As I told him what I'd done, he began to chuckle. "Azaleas need a little acid in the soil," he said. "Regular potting soil is perfect for ivy, but your azalea is starving to death."

How many times have you seen a similar scenario with couples at church? Plant a man and a woman in the same congregation. Same sermons. Same songs. Same programs. Same mission. She thrives, he withers and dies.

Sometimes this happens because the wife knows Jesus, and her husband doesn't. She's "abiding in the vine," while he's cut off. No mystery as to why he withers.

But I've noticed that even in marriages where both partners are genuine Christians, she often seems more devoted. Women just "get" church in a way men do not. As a result, nearly every church on earth attracts more women than men. Among Christians, women equal or surpass men in almost every category of religious devotion and participation.[1]

This shortage of men—is it a new phenomenon? Yes and no. The early church had no lack of men. Christianity's gender gaps have waxed and waned since the twelfth century. They became quite large in the Victorian era, but disappeared after World War II. Now the gender gap is growing again.

Why is this happening? Are today's men more sinful than women? Is God calling more women than men into his service? I've searched the Scriptures and can't find any evidence that one gender is more virtuous than the other. Adam and Eve both fell just as far.

Are men inherently less religious than women? No. Rival faiths welcome roughly equal numbers of male and female worshipers. There's no shortage of men in your typical Buddhist temple, Jewish synagogue, or Islamic mosque. And as I mentioned in the introduction to this section, men have been the religious leaders of society since the dawn of civilization.

So that leaves us with one remaining possibility: There's something about church that's not connecting with laymen.

To return to our metaphor—churches are creating the ideal soil for women to grow, but it's making men sick. This is why the vast majority of church staff and volunteers are female.

Why 90 percent of U.S. men believe in God and 83 percent call themselves Christians, but fewer than 20 percent worship in a church on any given weekend.[2]

Adding to the mystery is the fact that some men absolutely love going to church. Pastors, for example. Worship leaders. Elders and deacons. That handful of committed laymen. If the soil is so toxic, why are these men thriving in it?

Let me explain with an illustration from the sports world.

Most basketball players are tall. Their skills and gifts match perfectly with a game whose target is ten feet off the ground. So in a manner of speaking, the "soil" of basketball is ideal for tall people. But not all the basketball greats are tall. There happen to be point guards in the NBA Hall of Fame who checked in at less than six feet tall—but they are few in number.

And so it is with church. The "soil" of church is ideal for many women. Feminine skills and gifts mesh perfectly with the culture of the church. Of course there are men who also possess these skills and gifts—but they are fewer in number.

The basic disconnect between men and church is not spiritual, it's practical. A lot of men feel incompetent in the house of God. Think about what we do in church on a typical Sunday morning:

- We sit.
- We sing.
- We listen to sermons.
- We hold hands and hug.
- We socialize.
- We go to classrooms.
- We sit in circles and share.
- We read aloud.
- We study.

- We care for children.
- We plan social gatherings, such as weddings, funerals, and potluck dinners.

Read that list again and ask yourself: Who would be more comfortable in these roles, me or my husband?

Most men know the truth: Their wives are much better at "doing church" than they are. Men realize they have little to offer, since their gifts and experience do not match the needs of their church. They feel unneeded, so they go passive or leave the church altogether.

Today's church offers the things women crave: safety, relationships, nurturing, and close-knit community. Women instinctively understand the unspoken rules of church culture: be nice, sensitive, cooperative, nurturing, and verbally expressive. Volunteer opportunities in the local church revolve around traditionally feminine roles: child care, teaching, music, hospitality, and cooking.

How did church get this way? Like a glove that gradually conforms to the hand of its wearer, church culture has subtly conformed to the needs and expectations of its most valuable demographic group: married women age thirty and older. Why are they so valued? These faithful women staff the Sunday school, sing in the choir, plan the events, and attend the meetings. Without their superhuman commitment, the ministry machine would grind to a halt. The key to a smoothly functioning church is to keep married women happy and volunteering.

As a woman, you probably don't notice anything feminine about your church. But men do. The moment they walk in they feel hesitant and out of place. Can they articulate their discomfort? Of course not—they're guys. They just know that church doesn't feel right, so they skip it—or go passive. Men are unwilling (or unable) to squeeze themselves into the feminine mold we expect of the modern churchgoer. Can we blame them?

You may be thinking, *Wait a minute. I've always believed the church is too male-dominated, harsh, and legalistic.* Sadly, some churches are led by male dictators, but far more common are comforting churches where the top priority is making everyone feel loved and accepted. We gather. We worship. We love one another. A lot of talking, but not much doing. Satisfying to you . . . boring to him.

And what about the men who lead our churches? We expect our pastors to be highly verbal, studious, and emotionally sensitive. We want pastors who are into relationships and who treat us with gentleness. In other words, churchgoers are happiest with ministers who possess so-called feminine gifts. Pastors who do not reflect these traits often find themselves unemployed.

So yes, males still dominate the top floor of Christianity. But just below this thin layer of professional clergy, women vastly outnumber men. No stripe of Catholic or Protestant church is immune. Leon Podles, who has written extensively about Christianity's gender gap, puts it this way: The church is an army of women led by a few male generals.

So this is what your husband isn't telling you: His religious reticence may have very little to do with God. He may simply feel unskilled, unneeded, or outnumbered in church. He may feel he has little to offer, and he has no interest in volunteering since most of the ministry programs are headed up by women.

Remember what we learned in chapter 4 about men and their boxes? Men tend to play with the boxes they are good at, while shying away from ones that make them feel incompetent. Men avoid church because it's a weekly appointment with incompetence. So your husband simply ignores the religion box. Or he leaves it to you.

Many men are so uncomfortable in their religion box they resort to self-protection at the mere mention of faith. They mock it. They dismiss it without examination. Or they fixate on some aspect of church they don't like. *There are too many hypocrites. It's all a bunch of superstitious mumbo jumbo. All they want is money. It's just a system for controlling weak-minded people. Priests are just sexual deviants.*

This self-protection keeps a man from having to be honest before God. With his heart safely locked away, he doesn't have to admit his neediness. He can deny his own sin because there's some hypocritical preacher out there who's worse than he is. Protector shields a man from the pain of his own spiritual shortcomings.

Remember those Old Testament stories about men being summoned before kings? If a man failed to present the king with an adequate gift, he was cast out or even killed.

Men today want to enter the presence of God. But most feel they have no gift to offer the local church. They can't preach, teach, or sing. They're not very good with children. Study and socializing are not among their passions. Sadly, the church is losing men because it tends to value the gifts found more commonly in women.

Sometimes a woman will challenge me on this. She'll say something like "Men don't hate going to church. My husband loves church!" I always ask, "Is your husband involved in the ministry there?" Without fail, these women answer, "Oh yes. He's in the _____ ministry."

Here's something your husband isn't telling you: He will only give his heart fully to an organization that needs him. Men must have something to offer—besides their money. When your husband feels valued and needed, and that his contributions are making a difference, then you will not be able to blast him out of the church with dynamite.

13

How Men Relate to God— and Church

A lot of women would be tickled pink if their husbands started coming to church. Yet they have no idea how to make that happen. They've prayed. They've cajoled. They've blackmailed. And nothing has worked. To their wives' consternation, growing numbers of *Christian* men are dropping out of church. These are guys who are walking with Christ but who find weekly worship attendance an exercise in frustration.

Obviously, if your man does not know God, he won't derive much joy from going to church. But here's something your husband isn't telling you: His religious zeal (or lack of it) may have very little to do with God. As we saw in the previous chapter, many men simply feel out of place in church—their skills and gifts are mostly unneeded there. And there are a number of other factors that influence a man's perception of who God is and how we humans should respond to him.

The reason your husband either hates or loves to attend worship today may depend on the experiences he had in church as a kid. Men who had a positive church upbringing are far and away the largest group of males involved in church today.

But a lot of men had negative church experiences in their youth. Your husband may be opting out of church because of something that happened in Sunday school thirty years ago.

Early in my marriage, Gina and I joined a church that offered adult Sunday school, but I refused to participate. This was scandalous to her, raised as a preacher's kid. Most Sundays she'd take a separate car and attend Sunday school; I'd join her later in the sanctuary for worship.

One Sunday after church she really got after me about this. "Why won't you go? It's a great class. A lot of your friends are in there. You're being a poor example to the kids," she said. I knew she was right, but I dug in my heels.

Later that week I was praying and God revealed the reason I hated Sunday school. I flashed back to my own fifth-grade Sunday school class. There were two boys who constantly picked on me. I was under attack in that Sunday school and Protector responded by convincing me that anything called *Sunday school* was dangerous.

Once I realized the truth, I was set free to return to adult Sunday school. After a couple of years I eventually worked up the courage to teach a men's class.

Thanks to early negative church experiences, men tend to develop a "spiritual inferiority complex." It starts when they see their mothers more devoted to the church than their fathers. Then they encounter Sunday school and youth group programming that's more suited to girls. In traditional, classroom-based Sunday schools, the girls usually win and the boys usually lose. That's because the rules are stacked against boys: Sit still, read aloud, memorize, find passages in the Bible, and receive instruction from a female teacher. Girls are usually better at these things than boys are.

Then there's the Christmas pageant. Sixth grade boys are forced to wear a fake beard and sing a solo in front of the whole church. I doubt this is what Jesus had in mind when he predicted men would suffer for his name.

So by the time they're adults, men are tired of being embarrassed in church. Experience has convinced them that women are just better at "doing church" than men are. It's not that young men are hostile to faith; they simply feel less qualified (or motivated) to participate in it. They'd rather leave religion to the experts: married women.

Some men get "inoculated" against Christianity as boys. They grew up in dead churches that exposed them to a weakened version of the faith. This introduction is just enough to give them lifetime immunity from catching the real disease.

As a little boy, I remember sitting through lengthy church services wearing a stiff-collared shirt and choking necktie, my feet squeezed into uncomfortable patent-leather shoes. By the age of seven, I had come to associate church with physical discomfort and boredom. I decided then and there I was going to quit church as soon as I was old enough.

Teenage boys are desperate to prove their manhood. This is why they engage in so many risky, dangerous behaviors. Unfortunately, modern Christianity is marketed as "safe for the whole family"—and Jesus is something of a sissy. Churchgoing is the polar opposite of the dangerous image young men want to present. Here's something your husband isn't telling you: He's not ashamed of his faith, but he has kept silent about it many times because he did not want to be perceived as weak, odd, or wimpy by his friends.

A lot of guys are afraid of God because they've been hurt by a man. That makes it hard for them to trust a masculine deity. A generation of men is growing up with deep father wounds. Simply put, men experience an emotional gash when they fail to receive the love and affirmation of their earthly dad. If a man grew up with an abusive or absent father, he may have a hard time believing he is loved and accepted by his heavenly Father. Psychologist Paul Vitz studied the lives of prominent atheists and found that in almost every case, they either grew up abandoned or abused by their fathers.[1]

Despite all these barriers, millions of men do find their way to church every weekend. What are the things that bind men to a local church? In the previous chapter, I revealed the big number one: a feeling of being competent, wanted, and needed. But there are a host of other reasons men choose or reject a particular congregation.

Let me share a little secret even men don't know about themselves: If a man likes his pastor, he likes his church. If he does not like his pastor, he does not like his church.

For a woman, pastoral quality is one of many variables she weighs when evaluating her congregation. But for men, it's all about the pastor.

When I ask men what they think about their churches, they don't talk about the facility, the programs, or even their friendships. The first thing out of their mouths is their verdict on the pastor. "I just love Pastor Ken; he's such a great guy." Or, "I can't stand that new pastor of ours; his preaching is so boring." Pastoral quality (both as a speaker and as an individual) is extremely important to men when choosing a church.

Women are different. They tend to choose their congregation based on relationships—they go where their friends and family go. Or they pick a church that offers a particular program they value (such as children's ministry). Women quickly build a network of relationships in that church, and that relational web binds them to it. Thus, a woman will remain in a church with lousy preaching because she can't abide the thought of leaving her friends. Men are the opposite—they will stay faithful to a church with lousy relationships because they respect the preacher.

Men don't follow religions, philosophies, or ideas—they follow leaders. If your husband looks up to the pastor, he will be much more likely to throw himself headlong into the work of the church. But if he disrespects the pastor, good luck getting him involved.

Studies have shown that men tend to prefer large churches over small ones. One reason may be that large churches offer quality. The sermons are interesting. The music is superb. Everything is done with excellence. Regardless of the size of the congregation, men want a church they can be proud to invite their friends to. But they will be reluctant to bring other men to a worship service that's homespun, corny, or half-baked.

One time I was leading a seminar in Oregon. I took a comment from a strapping fellow with a bushy beard and hands the size of dinner plates. "I own a construction company," he barked in a loud voice. "I'm always inviting my workers to come to church with me, but they rarely come. When they do come, they never come back." I asked him why. "I think it's the quality of the service. We have a small church and it's very family-oriented. We allow time for people to stand up and share. Our singers are not the best. We hold hands and sing a closing hymn. I like our church, but I think my friends see it as irrelevant to their lives, or kinda old-fashioned, or girly."

He continued, "A couple of years ago our church started doing mission work in Honduras. When I tell the guys what we're doing down there, they're very interested. One even wanted to donate. The guys 'get' mission—but they don't 'get' churchgoing."

Some churches are highly emotive—particularly "spirit-filled" churches. Here's something your husband isn't telling you: It's hard for him to become emotional in public.

Finish this phrase: "Big boys don't _____."

From a young age, males are taught to keep their emotions in check. Yet the moment a man walks into a charismatic church, he's expected to get happy for Jesus. I'm not speaking against emotion in worship. I'm merely pointing out that it's more difficult for a man to become visibly emotive in a public space than it is for you.

Now, here's a curious one: Surveys indicate that men tend to prefer "high-demand churches," those that enforce rules and standards. Men are not into crushing legalism or control-freak pastors, but they do prefer churches with a bottom line. Men tend to choose theologically conservative churches that base their teaching on the Bible. The National Congregations Study found self-described liberal churches were 14 percent more likely to have a gender gap than conservative ones.[2]

Men also prefer newly formed churches to long-established ones. So-called church plants have a grow-or-die ethos that men find attractive. Men's gifts such as strategic planning, bold vision, aggressive evangelism, and risk taking are welcome in a young congregation. But as a church matures it tends to take fewer risks. The membership stabilizes and giving firms up. Once a church becomes comfortable, you often see a subtle shift away from men's values toward women's values—relationships, nurturing, and close-knit community. Mature congregations focus on the people-in-here rather than the world-out-there. As a church turns inward men get bored and fall away.

Guys prefer upbeat music. Younger guys like contemporary worship tunes, except for those "love songs to Jesus" that portray the Lord as more of a lover than a leader. This is a bigger issue than you might imagine. Church music used to be quite militant—"Onward, Christian Soldiers"; "A Mighty Fortress Is Our God"; "Marching to Zion." Men loved those battlefield songs, but they've been replaced with "bedroom songs": "Beautiful One I Love"; "I'm Desperate for You"; "I Long for Your Embrace"; "Jesus, I Am So in Love With You." Men don't listen to love songs on the radio, and they certainly don't want to sing a romantic ditty to another man, even if it is to Christ.

As a result, men have stopped singing in church, particularly contemporary churches. It's true. I worship in churches all over America, and more than 80 percent of the men stand mute as the worship leader croons away on stage, telling Jesus how beautiful he is.

Men like to sing "doing" songs, but many of today's praise songs are "being" songs. The old hymns focused on our mission for God, but praise songs focus on our relationship with God. I know a number of guys who arrive late to church every week because they despise "Jesus is my boyfriend" music.

Happily, not all is doom-and-gloom when it comes to men and church. Guys are thrilled that church dress codes are passing away. For hundreds of years no man dared enter a church without suit and tie. But today most churches welcome people as they are, and men are particularly fond of this innovation.

One other thing men like about church is its recent embrace of technology. Most guys don't mind the big screens that have invaded the sanctuary over the past decade or two. Men tend to be visual learners, and they often remember what they see on the screen better than the words that flow from the pastor's mouth.[3] Churches that are big into technology tend to attract more men.

And I can't forget humor. Guys love to laugh in church. I'm not suggesting they are looking for a comedy club on Sunday morning, but I can tell you from personal experience that when men laugh they drop their guard. And when they drop their guard, God can more easily work in their hearts. Your husband realizes the gospel is serious business—but he appreciates a church and a pastor that don't take themselves too seriously.

When I ask men where they experience God's presence most fully, they rarely say "in church." Instead, they almost always mention an outdoor location. Lots of guys say they feel God's presence in the wilderness, on the ocean, or in the midst of a storm. "When I'm out hunting and I get up and watch the sun rise over the misty fields, God's presence is so thick I can almost touch it," said one man. Another said, "The time I really sensed God was when I was in a small boat that was almost swamped by a storm. As the waves came crashing over the bow I should have been panicked but I wasn't because I felt God as I'd never felt him before. I'd never felt so alive—or cared for."

Men have always found God outdoors. Read the great adventure stories of the Bible. With very few exceptions, God's power falls on men who are outside. Christians worship the God of the firmament; the God of the burning bush and the pillar of fire; the God who commands the wind and waves; the God whose son was born in an open-air stable and who died on Golgotha's hill.

So if your husband says, "I experience God much more on the golf course than I do sitting in a church building," he's probably telling the truth. Men experience God under an open sky. Why do you think so many young men receive Christ at wilderness camps? Why open-air stadium crusades are so effective at reaching men? Why churches still hold tent revivals when there's a perfectly good building sitting right next door? Men experience God's presence much more keenly outdoors. How else do you explain ice fishing?

Unfortunately, 99 percent of Christian worship and discipleship takes place indoors. This could be another reason we see more women than men in church. Maybe your husband doesn't go to church because he does not expect to find God under a roof.

Another place men report finding God is in the company of other guys. Some of the best spiritual conversations I've ever had erupted around a campfire when the cigars come out. Alaska men know this—they spend vacations not on some beach, but scrambling up the sides of mountains in search of animals to kill. They and their friends plunge into the wilderness, risking hypothermia, injury, mauling, and possible starvation to bag an animal. These men are not only acting out their ancient hunter role, they are searching for God—in the place he's always been. They're seeking the paradise garden Adam lost.

Men find God in adventure. I've known a number of nominal churchgoing men whose faith really caught fire after serving on a short-term mission team. Working for God in difficult conditions, depending on him every day for protection and strength is just the tonic for many men. It's one thing to read the Acts of the Apostles in the Bible; it's quite another to experience acts of God personally.

Men experience God more intensely in their hour of need. God's voice is harder to hear when things are cruising along and everything is going well. But when life is slowed by adversity, illness, or some other challenge, men come to the end of themselves. Faith in Jesus emerges when men admit the obvious—they cannot protect and provide adequately for themselves. They need God.

If your husband is undergoing a trial, this may be a sign that the Lord is calling him. So many Bible greats had their encounter with God in a moment of weakness or disability: Jacob (hip), Joseph (prison), Joshua (hiding), Jonah (whale), Samson (weakened), Paul (blind). These men found their calling not on a mountaintop but in the valley.

14

Why Your Husband Has a Hard Time Doing "Spiritual Stuff"

Note: This chapter assumes your husband is a Christian. If he's not, then the reason he doesn't want to do "spiritual stuff" with you should be obvious.

One time I asked a room of about a hundred Christian guys, "Be honest—how many of you regularly pray with your wives?" About a dozen hands went up. Then I asked, "How many of you would *like* to?" Almost every hand rose.

Even among highly committed Christian men, there's a reluctance to do spiritual stuff—even with their own wives. Men are constantly exhorted "to step up and become the spiritual leaders" in their homes and in the church. Yet very few are doing so. Here are some reasons men are reluctant to practice their faith at home:

Tradition. Some men grew up in homes where Mom took the lead in spiritual matters, while Dad was passive. Others grew up in a church where the women were the de facto leaders, and the only man who was truly living for Jesus was the pastor. If your husband has never seen a layman who leads his home spiritually, he may have no idea how to do it (or he may find the whole exercise strange and uncomfortable).

Some women don't want to be led by their husbands. Although a lot of women would love their husbands to step up as spiritual leaders, some resist. I spoke to one woman who thought the very idea was demeaning—or laughable. Like many, she was raised in a family where women took the lead in spiritual matters, and she couldn't imagine it any other way. When I suggested she step aside so her husband could take more of a leadership role, she felt insulted.

"I don't need anyone to lead me to God," she said.

"So if your husband is not your spiritual leader, what role does he have in the home?" I asked.

"He's my partner. We are co-equals before God."

"But in reality he's not feeling like your partner. He's stepping back and letting you be the leader," I said.

"Yes," she said quietly. "I wish he wasn't so passive in spiritual matters."

Here's something your husband isn't telling you: Most men don't really get the concept of "equal" the way you do. That's because men are hierarchical thinkers. Men ask, "Who is in charge of this?" Once they figure that out, they relinquish complete control to that person.

Men tend to put women in charge in these six areas:

- Child care
- Relationships
- Education
- Housework

• Health care
• Religion

Which leads us to the next thing your husband isn't telling you:

Many men feel ill-qualified to be spiritual leaders. Here we go again. I believe laymen fail to step up to leadership in the church and the home not because they are lazy but because they simply feel unqualified to do so. Blame it on that spiritual inferiority complex.

Most men feel their wives are more suited to be spiritual leaders. Why? Think of what spiritual leadership entails: a highly verbal regimen of Bible reading, book readings, bedtime prayers, and theological discourse. Men often think, *She's better at this stuff. Why not leave it to the expert in the family?*

Some women criticize or belittle their men's spiritual lives. I know of one man who had tried to lead his family in evening prayers, but his wife always took over because "he wasn't doing it right." I've heard of women who say to their husbands, "Why can't you pray like the preacher?" or "Why do you read so slowly?"

"Karen" was thrilled when her husband began leading family devotions. But she was more knowledgeable of the Bible, so she frequently corrected her husband's theology in front of the kids. Needless to say, he didn't lead devotions very long.

I've also heard women ridicule and patronize men's spiritual pursuits, saying things like, "You boys go off and have your little retreat; do your men's thing out in the woods." I know of one men's group in Florida that planned a guys' paintball night. Several key women went to the pastor to object. "Jesus is the Prince of Peace. How are firearms remotely Christian?" they sniffed. These women worried that the boys of the church might get the message that guns and the gospel were compatible. They demanded that the pastor shut down the event, which of course he did. You can imagine how mothered these men felt.

Praying aloud feels strange, religious, or artificial. In surveys men claim to pray nearly as much as women do, but what does your experience tell you? Does your husband pray as much as you do? Who's more comfortable praying aloud in public settings? How often does your husband willingly pray with you? And I hate to even ask this, but who is better at praying aloud, you or your hubby?

Once again, it's the spiritual inferiority complex that is silencing their prayers. I think a lot of guys feel their orations aren't long or fancy enough to be shared in public. Their prayers sound nothing like those offered by their pastors every Sunday. Pastoral prayers are focused, articulate, and polished. Laymen's prayers often sound stubby: "Hey, God, there's this problem I've got at work. Could you help me with that?" Because their prayers don't sound pious enough, men often self-protect by remaining silent.

I've participated in a number of mixed-gender Bible study groups. Most ended with prayer around the circle. Here's what I noticed: All the wives prayed aloud every week. But their husbands often chose not to. If they did pray, their prayers were usually short. And I hate to say it, but the wives sounded like professional pray-ers, while their husbands sounded like amateurs.

Whenever groups of men and women pray aloud together, the women almost always pray more. They pray longer. Their prayers are more eloquent and well formed. Why is this?

Studies have shown that women possess greater verbal fluency than men, thanks to their well-connected brains. And you may never have noticed this, but evangelicals use a strange language when they talk to God. I call it *prayer-speak.* Women and pastors are fluent in this language. Some laymen eventually master it after many years in church. But to your average guy, it's as foreign as ancient Greek.

Prayer-speak is a nonstop speech to God with frequent repetitions of his blessed, holy name, punctuated by the word *just*. I recently prayed with a woman who was fluent in prayer-speak. Read her opening statement aloud, as quickly as you can, and see if it doesn't sound familiar to your ears:

> *Father God, we just thank you for this day, blessed Father God, and we just ask you to be with us, Father God, and we just want to praise your holy name for the many blessings you bestow upon us, Lord, and Father God, we just ask you to touch us, Father God, touch us deeply, and Father God, we just come to you now, bringing our petitions before the throne of grace, dear God, and Father God . . .*

Different faith traditions have their own versions of prayer-speak. I grew up in a church that employed King James prayer-speak, which meant we talked to God as if he were still living in the age of Shakespeare. Pentecostals have a very aggressive form of prayer-speak, full of hallelujahs, shouts, and snippets of Scripture. Mainline ministers often adopt a highbrow prayer-speak, by draaaaaagging out voooooowels, speaking slowly and distinctly.

Now, I'm not accusing anyone of hypocrisy or deception. I realize that most prayer-speakers are sincere Christians who want to communicate with God. But prayer-speak is having an unintended side effect: It's literally intimidating men into silence.

"Geno" sits in church listening to longtime Christians communicating with God in prayer-speak. He thinks, *I'd like to pray, but I can't pray like that.* It's hard enough for Geno to have a conversation with someone who doesn't talk back (audibly). Requiring him to do so in a foreign dialect raises the bar too high.

You may be thinking, *Geno doesn't have to use prayer-speak. He can talk to God however he wants.* You know this. I know this. But Geno doesn't know this. He wants to fit in, and if the rest of the group uses a prayer code, he feels like a misfit when he can't match it. Rather than be embarrassed, he remains silent.[1]

And this is probably the main reason Christian men don't pray with their wives. We've built a mountain of expectations about what prayer should look like (kneeling by the side of the bed, heads bowed, eyes closed) and what it should sound like (blessed Father, we just praise your holy name, hallelujah!). If men felt comfortable talking to God like a normal guy talks to a friend, I think you'd see more of them praying aloud.

For years I resisted praying aloud with my wife. I'll tell you how we broke the logjam in chapter 17, which is full of ideas that can help free your husband to join you in "spiritual stuff."

SO WHAT'S A WOMAN TO DO?

Here's something you may not realize about women: You are born "improvers." You buy most of the self-improvement books. You have an entire cable network devoted to upgrading and decorating your homes. And what woman doesn't want to improve her looks?

But the one thing you love to improve more than anything is men. You spend years finding just the right one, and then immediately begin making him even better! Some gals treat their husbands like computer software: a product they buy once and then continuously upgrade. The title of a popular off-Broadway musical sums it up: *I Love You, You're Perfect, Now Change.*

It's only natural that some women see Christianity as a program that will help them improve their men. Their thinking goes like this: *If only my husband would allow God to work in his life, he'd stop smoking and cussing, tame his wandering eyes, and learn to control his temper. He'd put down the TV remote and take me on dates. These things will not only honor God—they'll make my life a lot nicer.*

Some women try to help God by nagging their husbands incessantly, trying to force them to change. Others drag their husbands into the church, which is supposed to function like a rock tumbler—knocking off his rough edges and delivering him back to his wife soft, polished, and pretty.

Here's something your husband isn't telling you: He hates being polished. Or redecorated. Or improved. Why do you think he moved out from under his mother's roof?

So if you can't remake your man the way you like him, how are you going to find happiness in marriage? Just grin and bear it when he screams at you? Turn a blind eye to his addictions? Pretend you're happy when he makes you miserable? No way. This is denial.

I've heard a lot of Christian teachers tell women in bad marriages to look to God for their fulfillment instead of their husbands. This is a rock-solid teaching I heartily endorse. The sooner you find your satisfaction in God and him alone, the sooner your soul will be at rest. This simple change in attitude has rescued many marriages and helped many women accept their less-than-perfect husbands.

But this teaching can also be taken the wrong way. Some women interpret it as, "So sorry you're trapped in an awful marriage. Just give up on your husband and turn to God. You don't need the love of an earthly man when you have the love of Jesus. As for your marriage, tough it out, sister."

Here's the truth about your husband: You probably already have a good man. But he's trapped in a cage of self-protection. As we've seen, just about every dysfunction common to men springs from his need to protect himself. He's devoting so much energy to surviving his wounds, he has none left to give to you and the kids. A man cannot reach out in love when his arms are clutched in a defensive posture across his ripped and bleeding heart.

Dear reader, your husband wants to love you more. He wants to protect you more. He wants to provide for you more. All the love and care you need are inside your husband. You just need a way to access it.

So ladies, here's the big secret to getting the man you want: Stop trying to improve him. Stop trying to fix him. Start trying to *free* him.

Let me say it again another way: Your job is not to reinvent your husband; your job is to help liberate him. Although Christ does the liberating, you can do your part to help the process along. That's what the remainder of this book is about.

15

Freeing Your Husband's Body

Okay, I know what you're thinking. *This is the chapter where Dave tells me to have sex with my husband every night, to talk dirty with him on the phone, and to greet him at the door wearing nothing but a smile.*

Sister, if these things sound good to you, please don't let me stand in your way. Sex is one of marriage's greatest gifts. It's meant to be one of the foundations of your relationship—not an accessory. Husbands and wives are supposed to be sexual and flirtatious with one another (have you read Song of Songs lately?). Frequency, passion, and creativity are all signs of a healthy marriage.

But in this chapter I'll be focusing more on the fundamental and less on the flamboyant. If your husband's basic physical needs are not being met, you won't have a happy marriage. But if his body is well cared for, you're more than halfway to winning the battle for his heart.

First, let me dispatch a quick misconception: A man's primary physical need is not sex. It's food. Your husband's drive to eat is more much more powerful than his drive to reproduce. If your mate isn't eating right, everything else goes out of whack.

Most guys don't really care what they jam down their gullets. As long as it's hot, filling, and somewhat edible, they are happy. Here's another thing you can blame on our ancestors. Hunting parties had to travel light, so they carried with them just a day or two of provisions. If the hunt took longer than expected, the men simply didn't eat. When they finally came upon food, they gorged themselves. They didn't care about nutritional value or even flavor.

Fast-forward to the twenty-first century. Men are still coming upon food and gorging themselves. And a lot of it's not very good for us. Our modern world is awash in cheap, calorie-laden convenience foods. This has led to a new problem the world has never known: widespread obesity, among both men and women.

Here's something your husband may never have told you: It means a lot when you prepare delicious, nutritious food for him. In fact, one of the main reasons he married you is because he was getting really tired of ramen noodles and Domino's Pizza. Rare is the man who wants to do all the cooking; most guys are grateful for a wife who prepares good food.

Why do men like women to cook for them? Anthropologists tell us that in every society on the planet, going back millennia, women have been responsible for preparing food and drink for their families. No society has bestowed this task primarily upon its men. Since the beginning men have brought home the bacon; women have fried it up in the pan.[1]

However, in our busy world, some women have lost sight of their ancient role. A lot of women work so hard they have little time to prepare or plan what their families will eat. And here's the reality: In most families, if the wife does not superintend the household diet, no one will. The men in your life will revert to their ancient habit of coming upon food and gorging on it, regardless of its nutritional value (if you've ever raised teenage boys, you know exactly what I'm talking about).

Please, no guilt trip here. I'm not suggesting you must spend hours slaving over a hot stove to make each meal from scratch.

Here's my point: Your husband wants you to take charge of the menu. Although some guys will assume this role, most will not. Women, I encourage you to take dominion over the food your husband and children eat. See it as a high calling to provide healthy sustenance to your loved ones.

Fortunately, there are lots of ways to skin this cat. Cook ahead and freeze food. Assemble ingredients and assign your teens to prepare the recipe. Healthy leftovers are great. Grocery stores now offer quick-fix foods that rival home cooking for nutrition and taste. Restaurants seem to be rediscovering vegetables. Even fast-food joints are offering a few healthier menu items.

I am so happy I don't have to worry about food—my wife takes care of that in our family. I'm a busy guy with two different careers—writing, and my day job. I love the fact that I can depend on her to make delicious, healthy food for me, so I can keep working. I want to be Provider, not Preparer.

In chapter 7, we learned that the male brain is intensely visual. Men actually get a cocaine-like shot of pleasure from looking at a beautiful woman. So here's your assignment:

Give your husband as many cocaine shots as possible. Satisfy his addiction by looking your best.

Here's something your husband hasn't told you: It's very important to him that you make an effort to look good. He likes it when you take care of yourself.

I know, Christians aren't supposed to care about looks. You may be thinking, *I want my husband to love me for who I am on the inside.* And he does. But he also wants you to look good on the outside. He wants the whole package.

I can hear the alarm bells going off in your head. Let me quickly slay the serpents that are whispering in your ear:

1. You do not need to look like a supermodel.
2. You do not need to be a size zero.
3. You do not need to have the finest clothing.
4. You do not need to cake on the makeup.
5. You do not need to change your hair color every month.
6. You do not need to obsess over your looks and your body.

Here's what your husband really wants: a wife who takes care of herself. A wife who makes the most of the looks she's got. And why are looks so important to men? Take a deep breath before you read this next paragraph.

Men compare. Men compete. Men size each other up by their spouses. When men arrive at a party, they scan the room looking at the various wives. And the man with the best-looking wife wins. All the other men secretly envy the man who's married to the goddess. *What a stud,* they think to themselves. They might even wonder what it would be like to have sex with her. (Sorry, we hate this about ourselves, but Provider just won't shut up!)

This explains why successful men put up with high-maintenance trophy wives. It's no fun living with a shrew. The payoff comes when other men look longingly at your wife and approvingly at you. Having a knockout wife raises your social standing at work, among your relatives, and even a bit at church.

Now before you vomit, don't women play the same game? Don't they compare themselves? Don't they gossip when another woman gains weight or wears a frumpy dress? Don't they spend billions annually on every conceivable beauty treatment? Don't they buy magazines festooned with pictures of hot women at parties? Don't they compete for male attention in social gatherings?

Anyway, back on topic. Your husband doesn't want to be married to an uptight supermodel; he wants to be married to you. But he wants to be married to the best-looking you possible. Here are some ways to give him that gift:

Dress nicely, in public and at home. Some women's household wardrobe consists of ratty sweatpants and ripped T-shirts. You don't have to wear pearls and pumps while doing chores, but would it hurt to put on a nice blouse? A woman who dresses shabbily around her husband is sending him a dangerous message: *If you want to see a beautiful woman, look elsewhere.*

Take care of your body. Too many women today are letting themselves go. Female obesity is at record levels nationwide (as is male obesity). A frustrated friend once told me, "My wife was trim when we dated. During our wedding reception I smashed a piece of cake into her mouth. She took that as her cue."

Why is it important to eat right and keep your weight under control? Here's the noble answer: Your husband loves you and he's genuinely concerned for your health. And here's the other answer: No guy wants an unappealing wife, for the reasons I've already mentioned.

I'm telling you this because your husband won't—especially if he's a Christian. Women are free to criticize their husbands' appearance (comb your hair, Ralph!), but if a man offers even the slightest negative opinion of his wife's comportment she's likely to shut him down. And as I mentioned, Christian men are not allowed to be concerned about how their wives look. Only inner beauty is supposed to matter. We even feel guilty for becoming sad when our wives get chunky. But we could never mention our frustration to our pastors or Christian friends, because we're expected to love our wives unconditionally. To admit our beloveds' burgeoning waistlines bother us seems carnal and unspiritual.

Shaunti Feldhahn found that 97 percent of men would willingly help their wives get in shape. These husbands would watch the kids, cook the meals, and spend money on exercise equipment or gym memberships if their wives wanted to work out.[2] Your physical appearance is that important to us.

Now, armed with this knowledge you have a choice. You can descend into depression over your weight or your wardrobe. You can be offended that looks matter so much to men. Or you can humble yourself and do your best to meet your husband's genuine need.

Now please, don't go too far the other way. A lot of women hate the way they look—even though they are quite pretty just as God made them. Fiona Macrae writes, "A survey of female students ages eighteen to sixty-five at British universities found that almost one in three would be willing to trade a year of their life in exchange for the 'ideal' figure of the likes of model Kelly Brook or actress Scarlett Johansson. The finding is all the more shocking because almost all of those polled were in the normal weight range—or even underweight."[3]

There's no need to put your plastic surgeon on speed dial. I'm not talking about weekly Botox or $400 hair appointments. In fact, most husbands would prefer you not spend a fortune on body treatments. Hubby gets tired of your constantly changing your hair, wardrobe, and purse in search of the perfect look. Just take care of yourself. Find a style that pleases you both and stick with it. 'Nuf said.

～

Now it's time to talk about that other great physical need your husband has. Sex. I'm not a doctor or sex expert. I'm just a husband. So I'm going to keep this simple.

First, realize that sex is one of the cornerstones of the male psyche. If a man has a satisfying sex life, everything is right with the world.

Perhaps you've seen the TV commercial for Viagra, starring a middle-aged executive strolling confidently through his office. His co-workers call out, "Hey, Joe, you look great." "Hi, Joe, you been working out?" "Hey, Joe, is that a new suit?" Of course, the viewer knows why Joe looks so self-assured—he's performing in the bedroom, thanks to Viagra.

While we're on the subject of TV ads, have you seen the ones for Cialis, another sexual-enhancement drug? The couple begins caressing in the kitchen and soon the world is melting away behind them. A man must have written that ad. That's *exactly* what lovemaking is like for me. Everything else fades. It's just my beloved and me. There's an intimacy I can't even begin to describe. Lovemaking turns off the noise in my head. It sends Protector and Provider out for a coffee break.

In case you hadn't noticed, one of the best ways to diffuse tension in your relationship is by making love to your husband. You may not want to have sex with a man who's in a bad mood, but there's no better way to get him into a good one. There's no sin in using sex to make your life more pleasant. Your husband certainly won't mind.

Here's something else about sex your husband hasn't told you: It's his greatest source of comfort. Sometimes it's the only way he can access the emotions trapped deep in his heart.

I know a man whose favorite hunting dog had to be put down. Both he and his wife loved that animal. She cried the whole way home from the vet, but he was silent. She tried to get him to talk, but he just stared into the distance. When they got home she took his hand, led him into the bedroom, and made love to him. As they reached climax, tears exploded from his eyes. He sobbed and sobbed until he was emotionally spent. The man later told me it was one of the kindest things anyone ever did for him. He was eaten up with a sadness men are not allowed to feel (after all, it's just a dog). The explosion that accompanies sex helps a man express his deepest feelings.

Lovemaking is like magic pixie dust for your husband's soul. Sex makes everything better. It's like an emotional reset button. I've gone to bed loaded down with worries, problems, and cares, but after my wife and I come together everything seems doable. What were mountains are now molehills.

Now I'm going to share with you the single most important thing you must understand about your husband's sex life. You may know this already, but in case you don't, here goes: The key to his enjoyment is your enjoyment. In other words, if you are enjoying sex, he's enjoying sex. But if you're zoned out, stressed out, or faking it, he'll be frustrated. It's all about pleasing you.

No pressure, ladies.

When it comes to sex, men are into quality over quantity. Surprised? Shaunti Feldhahn's survey revealed that 97 percent of men felt it was important to be wanted and desired by their wives. Only 3 percent would be satisfied by quantity of sex alone. And only a quarter of men would be happy with a wife who offered all the sex he could want, but who did so reluctantly or out of a sense of duty.[4]

Your enthusiasm = his joy. You've got to want him. If you're into it, he's into it. If you're counting the ceiling tiles, he will remain unfulfilled.

You have to learn how to turn off your rational mind and fall over the cliff with him. Different couples have their ways of setting the mood. Music. Soft lighting. Perfume. A glass of wine. Whatever it takes to unplug from your life and responsibilities, do it for your husband. He can usually tell if you're acting. There's no sense faking an orgasm; instead, learn what gives you a real one and tell him how to make it happen.

That brings up another point: Don't make your husband guess about what pleases you. Tell him. Don't be embarrassed. He won't mind doing whatever it takes to pleasure you—because that's what pleasures him.

A lot of women bring sexual hang-ups into their marriages. Perhaps they were abused and associate sex with hurt and pain. Or they were taught from a young age that sex is dangerous or dirty. Christian girls who've lost their virginity as teens often bring needless guilt to the marriage bed.

If any of these describe you, I would highly recommend the services of a Christian counselor or sex therapist. The greatest gift you can give your husband is a wife who truly enjoys his affections. Honestly, there's nothing more foundational to his marital happiness.

Some women feel that certain sexual practices are out of bounds for good Christians. Here's God's rule for married sex: If your husband likes it, and you like it, then it's okay. Anything goes. Let me say it again: As long as it pleases both of you, *anything goes.* (One exception: using pornography as a sexual stimulant. Please don't go down that road.) If you try something and either of you doesn't like it, be bold and tell the truth. A good husband will be more concerned with his wife's pleasure than his own. My wife and I enjoy a great sex life after twenty-eight years because we've tried a lot of things. We know what we like and what we don't—and we're honest about it.

If you really want to thrill your husband, be the initiator. He'll feel as though he's hit the lottery. Here's why: Husbands generally want more frequent sex than their wives do, particularly in the early years of marriage. So they're often put in the position of having to ask for it. It's almost like a boy asking his mommy for a cookie. After a while, men begin to feel guilty about having to ask. So when you initiate, your husband knows the light is green. He feels confident, relaxed, and wanted.

Remember that old song from the classic rock band Cheap Trick? Your husband wants you to want him. He needs you to need him. He'd love you to love him. He's begging you to beg him. Take him aside and whisper into his ear, "Honey, I'm desperate for you. Will you please make love to me tonight?" Lay it on thick. Give him "the look" during dinner. There's no greater gift you can give him.

I can't end this chapter without addressing a growing problem: In some cases it's the man who refuses to have sex. I know of one wife whose husband stopped having intercourse with her after nine years of marriage. There was nothing physically wrong with him. He simply refused to initiate, and rebuffed her every advance. They continued to share a bed even as their relationship deteriorated. They're now divorced, each blaming the other for the breakup. Did I mention they met in church and were both Sunday school teachers?

A man's lack of desire can be caused by a number of issues. The problem can be erectile dysfunction. It can be a lack of confidence or low T level. He might be heavily into porn, masturbation, or an extramarital relationship that's releasing all the pressure behind the dam, so to speak. Or he might be angry with his wife about another matter, so he's punishing her by withholding sex. In some cases a wife may have closed the chocolate shop so often he loses interest. Or it might just be self-protection at work again.

Whatever the reason, it's highly abnormal for a husband to reject sex. Married sex is the best sex. We men are programmed to make love to our wives. Only a major glitch (physical or emotional) can disrupt that programming. In these situations it's wise to seek professional help.

You are competing for your husband's body. It's you versus a thousand foes—food, drink, drugs, illicit sex. Fight for his body and you'll win his heart.

16

Freeing Your Husband's Soul

Contrary to popular belief, the Bible is not chock-full of happy relationship advice. Whenever Jesus spoke of relationships, he usually predicted their demise (Matthew 10:34–35) or promised rewards for people who left their loved ones for the sake of the kingdom (Luke 18:29–30). Not exactly the kinds of things you hear on *FamilyLife Today*.

But there are a few verses in the New Testament that put a more positive spin on relationships. In fact, there's a clever guy by the name of Emerson Eggerichs who founded an international ministry and sold over a million books based on a single verse of Scripture:

> However, let each one of you love his wife as himself, and let the wife see that she respects her husband. (Ephesians 5:33 esv)

According to Eggerichs (and this verse), a woman's most basic need from her husband is love. But a man's most basic need from his wife is respect. Eggerichs asked seven thousand individuals this question: When you are in conflict with your spouse or significant other do you feel unloved or disrespected? Eighty-three percent of the men said, "disrespected." Seventy-two percent of the women answered, "unloved."[1]

You liberate your man's soul when you give him respect. When a man feels disrespected, he experiences the same pain you have when you feel unloved. Protector grabs his heart and shields it from that pain. Your husband cannot give you his heart because it's locked away in the cage. The man you truly love disappears and one of his survival strategies emerges: rage, drinking, silence, fear, control, and more. Then you resort to a survival strategy to deal with his dysfunction: nagging, codependence, arguing, manipulation, alcohol, and more. Eggerichs calls this "the crazy cycle."

How do you break this cycle? By showing your husband respect—whether he deserves it or not.

One time I was speaking to a women's group in Birmingham, England. As I was taking questions and answers, a well-dressed woman stood up and said, "I'll show my husband respect when he does something worthy of respect!" The other women whooped and hollered in agreement. After the hubbub died down, I said to her, "Respect is not something your husband is supposed to earn. It's a gift you give to him freely because God commands you to. I challenge you to show respect to your husband regardless of whether he's good or bad, kind or cruel. See if that does not change the dynamic in your marriage."

The simple act of giving men respect has saved thousands of marriages. Emerson Eggerichs's in-box is stuffed with testimonials from women whose marriages changed radically when they began offering unconditional respect.

When a woman fails to show respect to her husband, she poisons the relationship. She fails to meet his most basic need. When a wife speaks disrespectfully, calls her husband names, or embarrasses him in front of others, she may win the battle but will ultimately lose her marriage.

If a woman has been disrespecting her husband for a long time, it may take awhile to rebuild his trust. But each time she shows respect to her mate, he will feel a bit more secure. Protector will slowly lower his sword and open the cage. Her true husband will come out and play because he feels no threat—only her love and support.

Here are some specific ways you can show respect to your husband:

Appreciate him. Your husband gets beat up every day. Things go wrong at work. He gets stabbed in the back by co-workers. His boss mistreats him. His favorite sports team loses. His relatives freak out on him. His flight runs late. His car breaks down. His clients make unreasonable demands.

Sadly, the beatings continue when men get home. Shaunti Feldhahn found that just 23 percent of men said they felt actively appreciated at home. Meanwhile, 44 percent said they feel unappreciated at home.[2] Children are notoriously unappreciative of their fathers—particularly teenagers. A lot of wives never offer an ounce of appreciation to their husbands—they see only their shortcomings. Some women withhold appreciation until their husbands do something for them, sort of like a circus trainer holds back treats from an animal until it performs a trick.

When a man feels unappreciated, he starts to entertain crazy thoughts. Here's a voice that whispers to me when I feel unappreciated: "My wife and kids are so ungrateful. They never notice all the things I do for them. I work so hard to provide them with everything, and all they do is complain. I ought to leave them! Then they'll finally appreciate me.

I mean, what if I got cancer and died? Then they'd finally realize what a great guy I am."

I'm not alone in feeling this way. A lot of men abandon families they love simply because they feel unappreciated. They meet another woman who says those magic words, "I appreciate you. I want you." They're willing to go through the hell of a divorce, child custody, and alimony, turning their backs on families they love because their need for respect is so deep.

If you want a happy husband, turn your home into an oasis of appreciation. Point out the things he's doing well. Thank him. Find at least one thing to appreciate about your husband every day. Tell him with your words, with your smile, and with your physical affection that you appreciate him. Get him into the habit of coming to you for appreciation—instead of to his job, his hobbies, or his old girlfriends on Facebook.

Appreciate your husband not only to his face but also behind his back. Some wives run down their husbands in front of the children. Or when their teenage children rag on Dad, they nod in agreement. This mutual griping binds the children closer to you (you win the battle), but it marginalizes your husband (you lose the war). Eventually the whole family begins disrespecting Dad in subtle ways. This causes Dad to withdraw emotionally because he gets tired of being the bad guy—or the fool.

It's also very important that you speak respectfully about your husband among your friends. My wife tells me women love to swap my-husband-is-worse-than-your-husband stories. Christian women sanctify their spouse bashing by delivering it in the form of a prayer request: "I need you to pray about my husband. He comes in from work and just parks in front of the TV. We haven't had a date in months. It's driving me crazy!" This is not to say you should never share your frustrations about your husband with anyone else, but be careful to do so respectfully.

Trust him—even in those situations where you think you know better than he does. Women tend to trust themselves implicitly when it comes to relationships. They often believe their approach is the right one, while their husband's is the wrong one. Sorry to pick on my wife again, but she used to be really bad about this. Here's our story:

My wife, raised as a preacher's daughter, learned at an early age to be very diplomatic with her speech and to manage the truth so no one's feelings would be hurt. On the other hand, I'm a very bold, plainspoken sort of guy. As such, I sometimes put people off. My wife noticed this tendency early in our marriage, so she began administering my relationships and conversations for me.

For example, any time I spoke to her parents she would serve as a translator, smoothing out and clarifying my words. Before I spoke to relatives on the phone she would coach me with what to say and how to say it. She would manage my conversations at church, quickly reinterpreting my words if she thought they had the potential to offend. She even set herself up as an intermediary between the kids and me. They came to her to find out what I was thinking, and I would go to her to find out what they were thinking. All this was to ensure my relationships ran smoothly under her expert supervision.

Remember, when a woman takes control of something, a man immediately backs off. After a few years of having my relationships professionally managed, they began to atrophy. I enjoyed a strong bond with my wife (since everything went through her), but I was becoming estranged from my children. Her parents lived with us, but I could hardly carry on a conversation with them. I began to go silent in social situations and let my wife do all the talking, since she was just going to rephrase everything I said anyway.

You would think I'd be angry about this. But here's the strange thing: I didn't even notice it was happening. It had been going on so long it just seemed normal.

But Gina noticed something was wrong and began to express her concerns:

"David, you don't say anything in social gatherings."
"You seem withdrawn from the family, absorbed in your computer screen."
"You don't ever spend time with friends anymore."
"You have a scowl on your face most of the time. People are afraid to approach you, even at church."

We eventually landed in joint counseling, and for the first time, we both saw what was really happening. Subconsciously, I was angry at her for managing my relationships. She had no idea she was doing it. I forgave her, and she began trusting me to tend my own relationships. With Gina out of the middle of our family, all our relationships have improved. The smile is back on my face—and our marriage has never been stronger. And as a bonus, I'm learning to become more gentle and compassionate in my speech.

Another area where women trust themselves and not their husbands is with conflict resolution. Men often prefer to take the bull by the horns, but women usually prefer a gentler way. Women are natural peacekeepers. They often see their husbands as ungodly when they chew someone out or take a tough line disciplining the kids. They never even consider the possibility that a little righteous anger might be just what's needed to clear the air. Remember, Jesus was bold in conflict—more often a lion than a lamb. You need to trust your husband even when he handles a situation more assertively than you would.

Smile. A woman's smile is her most powerful tool. Why? Let's go back to infancy again. When your husband looked up and saw Mommy smiling at him, all was right with the world. But when Mom stopped smiling, he braced himself for the worst.

Therefore, being smiled at by a woman is one of the most pleasant things that can happen to a man. When I was a young buck, ladies used to smile at me all the time. Now that I'm in my fifties, they pretty much ignore me, unless they're working for a tip. I must confess I will often choose a female checker at the grocery store just for the thrill of being treated kindly by a woman.

One of the most encouraging things you can do for your husband is to smile at him. Consistently. Regardless of whether he's been a good boy or not. Show him God's grace with your face. You'll be amazed at the effect it has on your man. A consistent smile and a supportive attitude is soft power at its very best.

Believe in him. Sadly, a lot of women don't believe in their husbands. I have a friend with a big dream, but it would require him to move his family to a distant state. His wife is absolutely dead set against it because it would require her to leave family and friends behind. She is well established in the community. Her parents live nearby. So instead of telling him her fears directly, she ridicules his vision. By belittling him and his dream, she gets what she wants—but her marriage suffers.

Men with big dreams inevitably face disappointments along the way. When your husband comes home looking like he's been dragged through a cornfield, don't tell him, "I told you so." He needs an encourager—not a judge. If a man's wife does not believe in him, neither will anyone else.

Of course, many women do believe in their husbands. My very optimistic wife always encourages me to pursue my dreams. I hardly need to seek her advice because I know she'll always say, "Go for it!"

Need him more. One of the kindest things you can do for your husband is to make him feel needed. Dr. John Gray writes, "Men are motivated and empowered when they feel needed. Women are motivated and empowered when they feel cherished."[3]

So how do you make your man feel needed? Simple. Ask him to do things for you.

Modern women have been taught that it's wrong to rely on a man for anything. They've become too independent, making their men feel useless in a relationship. Allow your husband to serve you—and express your gratitude. Let him pick up the check. Ask for his advice. Get him to open the pickle jar. Men love to be useful and appreciated.

Caveat: Men love to be needed, but they recoil from neediness. Men are not looking for a clingy, whiny wife who's in constant need of rescue. That's codependence.

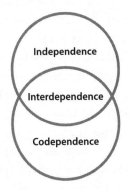

Interdependence is the sweet spot for men. They want to serve and be served. They want to depend on you and they want you to depend on them. It's all a part of becoming *one.*

180

Next, I'm going to share the secret to getting your husband to do exactly what you want. This amazing method works with all kinds of men. Are you ready? Here goes:

1. Get his undivided attention.
2. Look him in the eye.
3. Tell him clearly and unambiguously what you want.

That usually does the trick. If it doesn't, ask him again. Be nice about it. Don't nag—that just makes him mad. Not surprisingly, nagging is correlated with marital unhappiness and divorce.[4]

What's the difference between nagging and asking multiple times? The attitude of the one doing the asking. Most men appreciate a friendly reminder—as long as it's friendly. If you come across as pouty or disappointed, that's nagging.

Above all, don't make your husband guess what you want. Tell him clearly. Don't expect him to read your mind.

Women have this romantic idea: "He should just know what I want." (Cue: the chirping birds, rainbows, and unicorns.) It's as if love magically imbues a husband with telepathic powers.

"He should just know." What a load of baloney. This attitude will strain your marriage and stress out your husband.

Back in our pre-counseling days, my wife used to play this little game with me. See if it sounds familiar:

> *Me: Honey, what restaurant do you want to eat at tonight?*
>
> *Gina: It doesn't matter, you pick.*
>
> *Me: How about Mexican?*
>
> *Gina: Okay.*

So we'd go out for Mexican food. And the rest of the night I was married to the White Witch of Narnia. Silent. Cold. Imperious.

What went wrong? She wanted Chinese, and I'd failed to read her mind. So she punished me for it, ever so subtly.

> Me: *Honey, how's your chimichanga? You've hardly touched it.*
> Gina: *Fine.*
> Me: *What's wrong?*
> Gina: *Nothing.*

This is actually a game she learned from her mother. Here are the rules: Wives of the 1960s were never supposed to speak directly about their wants. That would be considered pushy. Instead, they gave their husbands subtle clues. Then, based on those clues, the husband was supposed to guess what she wanted. If he guessed right, that meant she was truly loved. If he guessed wrong, she was allowed to pout, as a consolation prize.

Here's what Gina was expecting: She had sent me a clue that she didn't want Mexican food. By answering with a simple, "Okay," she was hinting that I was supposed to look deeply into her soul and divine her true feelings about dinner. It turns out she was feeling bloated that night, and I was being insensitive by suggesting a high-calorie meal. She didn't tell me this—I was "just supposed to know."

Put yourself in my shoes. I think I'm getting gold stars for taking her out to dinner. But she's upset because I didn't get her what she wanted. I offered her a gift of love. She focused on what was wrong. And here's the message I received: *Don't even try to love me this way, because if it's not perfect I'll be upset.*

All this unpleasantness could have been avoided if my wife had simply spoken up and said, "I'm in the mood for Chinese." Mongolian beef or tacos al carbon—it didn't matter to me. Happily, after years of begging my wife to speak up, she's finally learned to do so. This has made both of our lives so much more pleasant.

Women, give this gift to your husband. Tell him exactly how you feel. What you want. Don't expect him to guess. And don't punish him if he can't read your mind. Tell him you want flowers this week, and then be happy when they arrive. Good husbands are not born, they are trained.

Respect yourself. Ironically, one of the best ways to respect your husband is to stand up for yourself. Don't be his doormat. Here's a little secret: Men love strong women. But they despise a gal with no backbone.

Some women, in an effort to be submissive, completely subsume themselves. They cede all power to their man, placing him on the throne and crowning him king. This is the worst thing you can do for your husband. It completely upsets the balance in a relationship. And here's something your husband isn't telling you: Even if he is tyrannical at times, he does not want to be a tyrant.

My father used to terrorize our family with his rages. My mother was a classic middle child who always tried to soothe and defuse the situation. The more submissive she became, the angrier he got. But once in a while a remarkable thing happened—Mom stood up for herself. She faced Dad down. He would explode, but within a few minutes he was calm again.

If you're the codependent type of woman who's "too nice" and your husband runs roughshod over you, it's time to grow a spine. Speak up for your needs. Tell him how you really feel. If you disagree with him, say so. If he is mistreating you or your relationship, follow the procedure outlined in Matthew 18.

Some sick men use the doctrine of submission to abuse their wives and children. Don't be a victim. Paul commands wives to submit—and husbands to love. That's the bargain. Your husband deserves a submitted wife and you deserve a loving husband who sacrifices himself for you, just as Christ did for the church. (See Ephesians 5:22–27.)

I'll say it again: No man wants to be a tyrant. Rage comes from the little boy trapped inside the cage, hurting over what was done to him long ago. Your husband wants to grow up into a responsible man—and you can help him by being strong. You show your husband respect not when you cower before him, but when you hold fast to the truth, and speak it in a respectful way.

———

Laura Munson wrote about the day her husband walked up to her and said, "I don't love you anymore. I'm not sure I ever did."

He expected her to burst into tears. To rage at him. To threaten a custody battle. To beg him to change his mind. She did none of these things. Instead, she looked him square in the eye and said, "I don't buy it."

So he got mean. He called her names. He asked for a divorce. She stood her ground. She was married—and that was that.

He said he wanted to move out. She didn't panic. She asked, "What can we do to give you the distance you need, without hurting the family?"

This made him even madder, but he didn't move out. He spent the better part of a year being irresponsible. He missed family gatherings. He was distant. He refused to look Laura in the eye.

But over time he slowly began to return. He started mowing the lawn. He began talking about the future. He ordered some firewood. At Thanksgiving, he offered a brief prayer: "I'm thankful for my family."[5] Over time her husband came back. And they're still together.

By standing firm, Laura Munson set her hurting husband's soul free. She did not achieve this miracle by exerting hard power (hiring a lawyer and kicking him out) or by manipulating (whining and crying) or by guilt ("Think about your children!") or by taking the blame upon herself. She did it by holding fast to a simple truth: She was married, and she was determined to show her husband respect, even when he did not deserve it.

17

Freeing Your Husband's Spirit

'm going to keep this chapter very brief. I've already written a full-length book on this very topic: *How Women Help Men Find God*. If you're really serious about introducing the men in your life to Jesus (and the church), I recommend you pick up that book.

As we learned in part 4 of this book, men often shy away from church because of the spiritual inferiority complex. They tend to see women as being more qualified in religious matters. A lot of men grew up in matriarchal churches, or in homes where their mothers were the true spiritual leaders.

Men resist God and church for the same reason they resist anything: self-protection. Men naturally avoid the things they're not good at. Masculine gifts are not wanted in most churches. So they pour their energies into activities they are skilled at.

Of course, sin plays a role. A lot of guys know their lives don't measure up to God's standards, and they are not ready to repent. So they skip church out of a misguided sense of integrity: They wouldn't want to become hypocrites themselves.

⸺

So what's the best way to free your husband's spirit? As we learned in the previous chapter, your husband needs to feel competent, respected, and needed in the kingdom of God. Once he learns that church is not a dangerous place, he'll stop avoiding it. Protector will put down his sword and your husband will be free to explore his spiritual life. Here are some ways you can assist:

Don't "fall in love" with Jesus or his church. Modern Bible teachers encourage women to "fall in love" with Jesus—and some women are taking this metaphor literally. Linda Davis writes, "All he knows is that she's in love with someone else, and he is jealous. Instead of remaining the first priority in her life . . . he has suddenly been demoted to number two after God."[1] Men respond to Christ as they would to any other rival—by fighting back with resentment toward the church.

Sabrina Black recalls a time when she returned from church to her husband's withering stare. "If I want anything done around here, all I need to do is call the church and let your pastor tell you because you do what the pastor says to do," he told Sabrina. "When the pastor says he needs somebody, you come running. When the pastor says there is a committee or a project, you show up. If I ask you to do something, you are too busy."[2]

A lot of women fall into this trap because they get so much affirmation for their church work—affirmation they may not be getting at home. Men are not the only ones who gravitate toward whatever cheers them on.

Your husband is not more important than God—but he is more important than your religious routines. Leslie Strobel scored points with her then-atheist husband by putting away her Bible and greeting him warmly whenever he came into the room. She wasn't hiding her faith. She was simply communicating to Lee that he was more important than her personal piety. Eventually Lee became a Christian and is now one of the world's best-known apologists for the faith.

Don't outshine your husband in spiritual matters. One time Gina and I led a couples' Bible study in our home. Eduardo and Rita were regulars. One time I asked Eduardo to look up a verse. When he couldn't find it quickly enough, Rita took the Bible from him and—with a dramatic sigh—found the passage in less than ten seconds. She handed the Bible back to her embarrassed husband with a look of triumph. Rita had used God's two-edged sword to publicly emasculate her man.[3]

Then I learned the rest of the story. Eduardo was a very critical husband. Though he was quite charming in public, he constantly belittled his wife at home. Rita saw this as her chance to get even with Eduardo—and to make *him* feel like the dummy.

Rita won the battle, but she lost the war. Eduardo never returned to our group. Eventually he left the church. The marriage was destroyed. I'm not saying this single incident was the cause, but the enemy used it to cut off Eduardo from his best source of Christian fellowship and support.

Women, you must never use your spiritual superiority to get even with your husband. Instead, follow the command of Paul: "Do nothing out of selfish ambition or vain conceit. Rather, in humility value others above yourselves" (Philippians 2:3–4). This is the heart of submission: Treat your husband as a better Christian than yourself, even if you're more skilled in faith practices.

Pray with your husband. Would you like your husband to pray with you? Most women would. Yet few couples consistently pray together—even those who attend church regularly. Pastor Larry Keefauver writes, "For the hundreds of times I heard wives sigh, 'I wish my husband would pray with me,' I rarely hear any husband express that desire."[4]

As you might have guessed, it's that good ol' inferiority complex again. As we saw in chapter 14, Christians speak normally to one another, but when they speak to God they lapse into a special language I call prayer-speak. Thanks to their highly verbal brains and prayer-speak fluency, women literally intimidate their men into silence.

For years, this insecurity kept me from praying with my wife. Oh, we tried. We would kneel by the bedside. There would be a brief period of silence, and then it began. My highly verbal wife would engage her church-trained tongue, gushing a torrent of words toward the heavenly throne. Five or ten minutes would elapse with hardly a breath, comma, or period.

Then, silence. It was my turn. As a man, I felt I had to match her length and intensity. I could never do it. My prayers felt short and stubby after my wife's lengthy epistle. Deep in my heart I felt outclassed. So I gave up.

After many years of prayerless frustration, Gina and I got to the bottom of it. She learned to start her prayers in silence, always giving me the first word. When it was her turn, she matched my length and cadence. If I prayed ten words, she prayed ten words. This changed our prayer life. Now, instead of lifting lengthy speeches to God, we go back and forth, offering a brief sentence or two. Then we wait for the Spirit's prompting before speaking again. I no longer feel inferior.

One more thing: My wife and I have begun salting our daily conversation with spontaneous prayer. We talk to God as a third person as we're walking or driving or shopping. No eyes closed or head bowed. Your man may be more willing to pray if he can do it on the spur of the moment, as the Spirit leads. Example:

Gina: *Hey, I heard from my Aunt Peggy. She's not doing well.*

David: *What's the matter?*

Gina: *Her medication is messed up. She's feeling very sick.*

David: *Lord, please help Aunt Peggy. Help the doctors get her medication adjusted.*

Gina: *Yes, Father, she really needs your help.*

David: *Hey, honey, what about Uncle Danny? How is he doing?*

Gina: *Oh, he's great. He's the one who called me . . .*

Dear reader, it's all about competence and confidence. The men who love church and spiritual pursuits are the ones who have something to offer. If your husband has a skill or passion, see if there's some way he can deploy it at church.

Joanne was a faithful churchgoer. Her husband, Nate, was a computer nerd who refused to attend except at Christmas and Easter. One Sunday, Joanne asked her pastor, "Could the church use some periodic help with the computer network?" Her pastor said, "Boy, could we, but tech support is so expensive." Joanne went home and mentioned the need. To her surprise, Nate offered to help. He began volunteering once a month in the church office, installing updates, zapping viruses, and hooking up hardware. One day the pastor took Nate to lunch, as a thank-you. The two men hit it off. Next Sunday, Nate and Joanne were sitting together in church. He's been going ever since.

Men will go to church when they feel safe there. When they feel competent. When they have a gift to offer. And most important, when they have a friend who leads them. Men follow pastors they respect and friends they admire. Do whatever you can to get godly men into your husband's life. Proverbs 27:17 (ESV) says, "Iron sharpens iron, and one man sharpens another."

There's much more you can do to encourage your man's walk with God. For more information, visit my website for women, www.speakingofmen.com.

Conclusion

A More Perfect Union

Husband: *Did you pick up my suit at the cleaners?*
Wife: *I'm sorry.*
Husband: *You never listen, do you?*
Wife: *Hey, I've got a lot on my mind.*
Husband: *Well, I'm certainly not on your mind.*
Wife: *That's not true.*
Husband: *You've got a memory like a sieve.*
Wife: *Hey! You've got a car. Get your own suit!*
(storms out of the room).

Have you noticed that when couples fight, the issue is rarely the issue? The smallest rain cloud can produce a thunderstorm between spouses.

My codependent parents used to fight over the silliest things: a lost checkbook, a late supper, which TV show to watch. They would have the same fight over and over—even repeating the same phrases. Dad would attack. Mom would defend herself or attempt to pacify him. But Dad could not be calmed, since he was not really angry about the issue at hand. He was angry about his past.

Dad had a very tough childhood. His parents divorced when he was three. He was sickly and spent a year in bed with rheumatic fever. He had some awful experiences in the army. Each time, Protector saved him from deep despair—but also locked a good portion of his heart away.

In many ways, my dad was a great guy—gregarious, generous, and loving, in an odd way. But when he was angry, he became a petulant child. He threw tantrums. His words were petty and illogical. Listening to my raging father was like hearing a ten-year-old arguing on the playground.

Now that I've visited the headwaters of my own soul, I understand what was up with Dad. Every few days the child inside him would rattle the bars of the cell. "Let me out!" he would scream. Dad couldn't literally say this, since he didn't recognize his own captivity. So the pressure built inside of him until he could contain it no longer. He fixated on something at hand and yelled about that. The issue was never the issue.

My father could have been freed. Jesus Christ held the keys, but Dad never knew it. Our family went to church for a few years when I was a little boy. Dad was even a Sunday school teacher. But one day Dad got mad at our pastor. We quit going to church. In all honesty, it probably wouldn't have mattered if we'd stayed. Our Lutheran congregation was into personal morality and charitable works. Churchmen of the 1960s did not know the conditions of their own hearts—much less how to liberate other men.

When you and your husband have conflict, recognize that his fury may not spring from the issue at hand. When his anger explodes (or smolders) over some small thing, recognize that his overreaction may be that of a captive young man calling for help.

Now, on the other hand, don't patronize your husband. Sometimes his pique is justified. If you overdraw the checking account twice a month, he has every right to be upset. Don't automatically dismiss his anger as the ravings of his wounded inner child. I'm merely saying that a lot of men's rage comes from their past; that doesn't mean he never has the right to lose his temper. Jesus lost his—quite often, in fact.

You'll never eliminate all conflict from your marriage. This is not a realistic or desirable goal. Conflict is healthy—if it's handled in the right way. You probably can't change the way your husband deals with conflict, but you can change the way you do.

Now I'm going to ask you to turn the camera onto yourself. You were hurt as a little girl. You also practice self-protection. You learned how to survive in your household: perhaps your tormentor was a teasing brother, an alcoholic father, a smothering mother. A lot of women bring their survival strategies into marriage as well.

Here's something you may not know about yourself: You see your husband through the lens of your father. You often react to him the way you reacted to Dad. And if you had no father, you may bring abandonment issues into your marriage.

I know one woman (let's call her Kate) who was raised by an angry father. The only time he showed her affection was after he had yelled at her and wanted to make up. She actually began to look forward to his outbursts because she knew that once he settled down she'd be basking in her father's love.

Kate grew up and married a very calm man named "Stu." She spent years picking at him, provoking him to anger, because this was the only way she knew how to get love from a man. Eventually, Kate hauled her husband into the counselor's office to find out why he was so angry with her all the time. In less than an hour, the counselor identified the core issue. Kate was horrified to learn the truth. She begged her husband's forgiveness. She immediately stopped needling Stu and learned to ask for his affection. Plus she gave Stu permission to call her up short if she ever lapsed into her old behavior. Their marriage was saved.

Even women with good, caring fathers learn negative habits from Dad. "Samantha" had a wonderful father, but he traveled a lot on his job. When she was eight she became very ill. Daddy rushed home to be with her. That incident taught her that being sick got her the attention of her father. For years, Samantha battled a host of psychosomatic illnesses. She brought this strategy into her marriage, always falling ill when her husband was preparing to be away. She had no idea her illnesses were imagined, despite getting a clean bill of health from three different doctors. It never occurred to her to speak openly with her husband of her fear of abandonment. Instead, she subconsciously resorted to her old survival strategy in a vain attempt to get what she needed.

Dear reader, if you want a more open and honest relationship with your husband, both of you are going to have to learn to stop playing these kinds of games. You must learn to speak up and ask for what you want. It may be easy to identify the ways your husband is self-protecting—but it takes courage to admit that you may be self-protecting as well.

Hear the promise of Jesus: "You will know the truth. And the truth will set you free" (John 8:32). Both you and your husband need to:

- Identify what hurt you in the past and how you learned to survive those wounds.
- Identify the games you still play to get your needs met.

- Learn to ask each other for what you need, honestly and openly.
- Give each other permission to "call the other out" the moment he/she starts playing games.

If every married couple could get to this point, books like this one would become unneeded. There would be almost nothing your husband would be unwilling to tell you.

Notes

Chapter 1: Understanding "Provider"

1. CBS News, "Survey: More Americans Unhappy at Work," January 5, 2010, www.cbsnews.com/stories/2010/01/05/national/main6056611.shtml.

2. CBS News Poll, "Where America Stands: The State of America and Its Future," Poll taken December 17–22, 2009, www.cbsnews.com/htdocs/pdf/poll_whereamericastands_010410.pdf?tag=contentMain;contentBody.

3. William J. Bennett, "Why Men Are in Trouble," CNN, October 4, 2011, www.cnn.com/2011/10/04/opinion/bennett-men-in-trouble/index.html.

4. Louisa Lim, "In Japan, 'Herbivore' Men Subvert Ideas of Manhood," NPR Morning Edition, November 25, 2009, www.npr.org/templates/story/story.php?storyId=120696816.

5. Tim Stafford, "The Anatomy of a Giver," *Christianity Today,* May 19, 1997, quoted at Generous Giving Research Library, http://library.generousgiving.org/page.asp?sec=4&page=161.

Chapter 2: Understanding "Protector"

1. The previous paragraphs contain some conjecture on my part. For the literal scriptural account, read Genesis, chapters 3 and 4.

Chapter 3: How Protecting and Providing Have Changed

1. Reuters, "Women vets now more likely to have seen combat: study," December 22, 2011, www.reuters.com/article/2011/12/22/us-defense-women-idUSTRE7BL0ZY20111222.

2. Centers for Disease Control and Prevention, National Center for Injury Prevention and Control, www.cdc.gov/violenceprevention/pdf/suicide-datasheet-a.pdf.

3. Hanna Rosin, "The End of Men," *The Atlantic* magazine, July/August 2010, www.theatlantic.com/magazine/archive/2010/07/the-end-of-men/8135/.

Chapter 4: Understanding the Male Brain

1. Bruce Weber, "Fewer Noses Stuck in Books in America, Survey Finds," *New York Times*, July 8, 2004, www.nytimes.com/2004/07/08/books/fewer-noses-stuck-in-books-in-america-survey-finds.html.

2. Mark Gungor, *Laugh Your Way to a Better Marriage* (New York: Atria, 2008), 42.

3. Ibid.

4. Amanda Lenhart, "Teens, Cell Phones and Texting," Pew Research Center, April 20, 2010, http://pewresearch.org/databank/dailynumber/?NumberID=991.

5. S. Craig Watkins and H. Erin Lee, "Got Facebook? Investigating What's Social About Social Media," November 18, 2010, www.theyoungandthedigital.com/wp-content/uploads/2010/11/watkins_lee_facebookstudy-nov-18.pdf.

6. Bill and Pam Farrel, *Men Are Like Waffles—Women Are Like Spaghetti* (Eugene, OR: Harvest House Publishers, 2001), 11.

7. Tom Davis and Tammy Maltby, *Confessions of a Good Christian Guy* (Nashville: Thomas Nelson Publishers, 2008), 119.

Chapter 5: Mr. T—The Stuff That Makes Your Man a Man

1. Andrew Sullivan, "The He Hormone," *New York Times Magazine*, April 2, 2000, www.nytimes.com/2000/04/02/magazine/the-he-hormone.html.

Chapter 6: Men and Sex

1. Occasionally an individual society chose to open some of the gates. Think of ancient Rome, or Corinth. Sexual taboos were lifted (at least in certain circles). Vice laws were relaxed. But the resulting wave of pregnancies, sexually transmitted diseases, and impoverished, fatherless children weakened these societies. Sexually libertine civilizations never endure long—they always rot from within.

2. To see a truly terrifying depiction of the sirens, watch the film *Pirates of the Caribbean III: On Stranger Tides*.

3. Jane Weaver, "Many Cheat for a Thrill, More Stay True for Love," MSNBC/iVillage Survey, April 16, 2007, www.msnbc.msn.com/id/17951664/ns/health-sexual_health/t/many-cheat-thrill-more-stay-true-love/#.TxcWtJj6S_c.

Chapter 7: What "Men Are Visual" Means

1. Shaunti Feldhahn, *For Women Only* (Sisters, OR: Multnomah, 2004), 111.

2. Itzhak Aharon, Nancy Etcoff, et al., "Beautiful Faces Have Variable Reward Value," *Neuron*, Vol. 32, 537–551, November 8, 2001, as reported in *Huffington Post*, September 30, 2011, www.huffingtonpost.co.uk/2011/09/30/a-beautiful-female-face-triggers-cocaine-effect-on-men-_n_988439.html.

3. Stephen Arterburn, *The Secrets Men Keep* (Nashville: Thomas Nelson, 2006), 220.

Chapter 8: His Soul's Greatest Need

1. John Gray, *Men Are from Mars, Women Are from Venus* (New York: HarperCollins, 2004), 56.
2. Farrel, *Men Are Like Waffles—Women Are Like Spaghetti*, 12.

Chapter 9: What Your Husband Is Afraid Of

1. Sam Keen, *Fire in the Belly* (New York: Bantam Books, 1991), 140.
2. Arterburn, *The Secrets Men Keep*, 82.
3. Tom Geoghegan, "Why Are Men Reluctant to Seek Medical Help?" *BBC News Magazine,* July 17, 2009, http://news.bbc.co.uk/2/hi/uk_news/magazine/8154200.stm.
4. "Pull the Other One," *Daily Mail,* May 25, 2011, www.dailymail.co.uk/femail/article-1390371/Women-sick-men-skip-work-soon-start-feeling-ill.html.
5. Erin Allday, "Women Found to Report Much More Pain Than Men," *San Francisco Chronicle,* January 23, 2012, www.sfgate.com/cgi-bin/article.cgi?f=/c/a/2012/01/23/MN681MSBB6.DTL&tsp=1.
6. *Kiplinger's Personal Finance Magazine,* "Unmasking 13 Financial Fears," October 29, 2004, www.kiplinger.com/features/archives/2004/10/fears.html.
7. Arterburn, *The Secrets Men Keep*, 2.
8. Lyle Alzado, "I'm Sick and I'm Scared," *Sports Illustrated,* July 8, 1991, http://sportsillustrated.cnn.com/vault/article/magazine/MAG1139729/index.htm.

Chapter 10: The Power Women Have Over Men

1. Belinda Luscombe, "Workplace Salaries: At Last, Women on Top," *Time* magazine, September 1, 2010, www.time.com/time/business/article/0,8599,2015274,00.html.
2. William J. Bennett, "Why Men Are in Trouble," CNN, October 4, 2011, www.cnn.com/2011/10/04/opinion/bennett-men-in-trouble/index.html.
3. Ralph Gardner Jr., "Alpha Women, Beta Men," *New York* Magazine, November 17, 2003, http://nymag.com/nymetro/news/features/n_9495/.
4. 1 Corinthians 7:3–5.
5. Sadie Gray, "Why Divorce Makes Women the Poorer Sex," *The Independent,* January 25, 2009, www.independent.co.uk/news/uk/home-news/why-divorce-makes-women-the-poorer-sex-1515463.html.
6. www.divorce-lawyer-source.com/faq/emotional/who-initiates-divorce-men-or-women.html.
7. John Tierney, "New Looks at Realities of Divorce," *New York Times,* July 11, 2000, www.nytimes.com/library/national/regional/071100ny-col-tierney.html.
8. U.S. Census Bureau, "Child Support—Award and Recipiency Status of Custodial Parents: 2007," www.census.gov/compendia/statab/2012/tables/12s0568.pdf.
9. Great Male Survey of 2011, AskMen.com, results published July 2011, www.askmen.com/specials/great_male_survey/.
10. "Poll: 9 Out of 10 Would Remarry Spouse," CBS News, poll conducted January 2012, www.cbsnews.com/stories/2010/02/14/sunday/main6207002.shtml.

Chapter 11: Why He Won't Share His Feelings

1. Warren Farrell, *Why Men Are the Way They Are* (New York: McGraw-Hill, 1986), 6–8.
2. Arterburn, *The Secrets Men Keep*, 59–60.
3. Willard Harley Jr., "Why Women Leave Men," www.marriagebuilders.com/graphic/mbi8111_leave.html.

Part Four: Understanding Your Husband's Spirit

1. Ernestine Friedl, *Women and Men: An Anthropologist's View* (Prospect Heights, IL: Waveland Press, 1984), 30.
2. David Murrow, *Why Men Hate Going to Church*, revised edition (Nashville: Thomas Nelson, 2011), xi.

Chapter 12: Why You Like Church Better Than He Does

1. *The Alabama Baptist*, "Women Provide Strength for Churches, Barna Finds," July 13, 2000, http://thealabamabaptist.org/print-edition-article-detail.php?id_art=701&pricat_art=5, accessed July 1, 2012.
2. Rebecca Barnes and Lindy Lowry, "Special Report: The American Church in Crisis," *Outreach* magazine, May/June 2006. Over a third of Americans claim to have gone to church during the prior week, but by studying actual attendance figures, the authors found that true attendance was about half that number.

Chapter 13: How Men Relate to God—and Church

1. Paul C. Vitz, *Faith of the Fatherless* (Dallas: Spence Publishing, 1999).
2. Dr. Mark Chaves, "National Congregations Study of 1998," University of Arizona. The study finds a gender gap in 57.9 percent of churches that characterize themselves as more conservative, 67.8 percent of churches that are right in the middle, and 72.4 percent of churches that identify themselves as more liberal.
3. George Barna, *The Second Coming of the Church* (Nashville: Thomas Nelson, 1998), 58.

Chapter 14: Why Your Husband Has a Hard Time Doing "Spiritual Stuff"

1. Murrow, *Why Men Hate Going to Church*, 192–193.

Chapter 15: Freeing Your Husband's Body

1. Frances Dahlberg, Introduction to *Woman the Gatherer* (New Haven: Yale University Press, 1981), 13.
2. Shaunti Feldhahn, *For Women Only* (Sisters, OR: Multnomah, 2004), 73.
3. Fiona Macrae, "The Women Willing to Trade a Year of Their Life for a Perfect Body," *The Daily Mail*, March 31, 2011, www.dailymail.co.uk/health/article-1371735/Millions-women-trade-year-life-perfect-body.html#ixzz1ldSNBLdc.
4. Feldhahn, *For Women Only*, 93–94.

Chapter 16: Freeing His Soul

1. Emerson Eggerichs's website, http://loveandrespect.com/.
2. Feldhahn, *For Women Only*, 68.
3. Gray, *Men Are from Mars, Women Are from Venus*, 43.
4. Elizabeth Bernstein, "Meet the Marriage Killer," *The Wall Street Journal*, January 25, 2012, http://online.wsj.com/article/SB10001424052970203806504577180811554468728.html.
5. Laura A. Munson, "Those Aren't Fighting Words, My Dear," *The New York Times*, August 2, 2009, ST 8: www.nytimes.com/2009/08/02/fashion/02love.html.

Chapter 17: Freeing Your Husband's Spirit

1. Linda Davis, *How to Be the Happy Wife of an Unsaved Husband* (New Kensington, PA: Whitaker House, 1987), 59.
2. Sabrina D. Black, *Can Two Walk Together? Encouragement for Spiritually Unbalanced Marriages* (Chicago: Lift Every Voice, 2002), 194.
3. Murrow, *Why Men Hate Going to Church*, 178.
4. Larry Keefauver, *Lord, I Wish My Husband Would Pray with Me* (Lake Mary, FL: Charisma House, 1998), xi.

David Murrow is director of Church for Men, an organization dedicated to restoring a healthy, life-giving masculine spirit in Christian congregations. His first book, *Why Men Hate Going to Church,* became a bestseller with more than 100,000 copies in print. He's spoken about the gender gap on the NBC Nightly News, Fox News Channel, and PBS, is a frequent guest on Christian TV and radio programs, and is a contributor to several Christian magazines, both print and online.

A sought-after expert and speaker on men's issues, Murrow spent twenty years honing his skills as a communicator, producing and writing award-winning television documentaries, commercials, and specials. He also served as director of communications for the Alaska governor's office.

Murrow has a degree in anthropology from Baylor University. He's a layman who's served as an elder in the Presbyterian Church (USA). He's married, has three children, and lives in Chugiak, Alaska. Learn more at www.churchformen.com, or his new site for women, www.speakingofmen.com.